THE STORY OF
BSA
MOTOR CYCLES

Bob Holliday
Foreword by Jeff Smith, MBE

 Patrick Stephens, Cambridge

By the same author

Norton Story
Motorcycle Parade
Motorcycle Panorama *(USA)*
The Keig Collection *(4 volumes)*
Racing Round the Island

Also in the same series

AJS: The History of a Great Motorcycle
by Gregor Grant
Norton Story
by Bob Holliday
The Story of Triumph Motor Cycles
by Harry Louis and Bob Currie
The Story of Honda Motor Cycles
by Peter Carrick
The Story of Kawasaki Motor Cycles
by Peter Carrick

In preparation
The Story of MV Motor Cycles
by Peter Carrick

First published 1978
Reprinted 1979

British Library Cataloguing in Publication Data

Holliday, Bob
   The story of BSA motor cycles.
   1. BSA motorcycle — History
   I. Title
   629.22'75   TL448.B2

   ISBN 0 85059 277 1

Set in 10 on 11 pt Times Roman type by Blackfriars Press Ltd, Leicester. Printed on Fineblade 100 gsm paper and bound in Great Britain by The Garden City Press Ltd, Letchworth, for the publishers, Patrick Stephens Ltd, Bar Hill, Cambridge, CB3 8EL

Contents

Acknowledgements

Many kind people and good friends have helped in the production of this book, with information, advice and assistance with illustrations. In expressing my overall gratitude I would like especially to thank Barry Palmer — 'Polly' to all members of the BSA Owners' Club — who provided the bulk of the photographs and catalogue material, as well as compiling the notes on which Appendix B is based. The Club is indeed fortunate to have such an enthusiastic, knowledgeable and co-operative Public Relations Officer.

Former BSA employees who have given unstinting aid include Harry Perrey (the Snowdon pictures came from his collection), Bert Taylor, Bert Perrigo, Ivor Davies, Brian Martin, Reg Dancer (the views of Armoury Road 1977 were taken by him) and Dennis Wood, who came up with the photo of his father aboard the 1921 TT racer.

I would dearly have liked to talk with Jack Sangster and James Leek but, sadly, Mr Jack died before I could arrange an appointment, and Jimmy Leek, now in his 80s, was not in sufficiently good health to grant me an interview. However, his one-time secretary, Mrs Allan Jones (née Gwendoline Arey) graciously and competently supplied much of the background information I was seeking.

Ivor Mutton, the Royal Enfield archivist, not only produced the original BSA engine drawings, but also photographed them for me, and S. R. Keig Ltd, the IoM photographic firm, provided TT pictures from their files. A number of general BSA views came from the National Motor Museum library at Beaulieu and the Birmingham Mail kindly supplied the picture of Bert Perrigo.

Keith Fletcher, whose antique bookshop in London's West End contains a wealth of motoring history, generously gave me the run of his shelves.

Appendix A, detailing BSA Clubman's racing performances, is almost word for word as it was written by that mastermind of TT statistics, John Greenwood, and Bruce Main-Smith's special interest in Gold Stars proved an invaluable aid.

For permission to reproduce Motor Cycle copyright material I am indebted to the editor of that journal, Mick Woollett, and for her typing skill I once again thank Joan Power.

And I am particularly grateful to Pat Stephens and his colleagues at Cambridge for their sympathetic forbearance when their publishing schedule was completely upset and delayed by an illness that hospitalised me mid-way through the writing of this story.

London, 1978   Bob Holliday

Illustrations

Diagrams in text

Foreword by Jeff Smith, MBE

When I joined BSA as a 16-year-old general engineering apprentice on a dull January morning in 1951, I was fulfilling an ambition that had grown since I was first exposed to motor cycles near the end of the 1939-45 war. Having the use of a variety of machines my favourite had become a 125 Bantam which had carried me to various successes and the odd failure in Midland Centre trials. By now, however, I was riding my father's 500T Norton and enjoyed the greater accomplishments which extra power brought within my reach. To work at BSA was to join the true world of motor cycles and, to the detriment of my technical schooling, I became totally fascinated in the preparation and riding of them, particularly competition machines.

Working as I did for the first two years of my apprenticeship at the Montgomery Street Service Department, I became familiar with the whole range of BSA machines, and while there advanced apace in my weekend pursuit of trials glory. So much so that by 1952 I was offered a works trials ride with Norton! The chance was too good to miss so I rode for one year, not too successfully, in the same team as Draper, Young, Breffitt and the immortal Duke. But that was only at weekends. During the week I crept through BSA's great carriage archway, passed the works' guard (who we always referred to as 'warders'!) and worked under the demanding eye of the service shop foreman, but in the company of an hilarious crew. They thought my riding for Norton and working at BSA a tremendous joke. But I always felt a little guilty especially as I passed the 'warder'!

At the end of 1952 Nortons disbanded their competition team and Bert Perrigo offered me the use of a Gold Star trials bike. Now began a relationship which was to last for almost 20 years and saw even the vaulting ambition of an 18-year-old surpassed by reality. Looking back down the years that first BSA was a wonderful machine, agile, docile yet remarkably boisterous and powerful when necessary. That in many ways described the company at that time. The plant was full of work and BSA was expanding with a sound business base. Motor cycles poured from the factory. The company was marching vigorously into the second half of the 20th century. Great captains of industry had her destiny in hand and no one could doubt that this great company would continue. Only gross and persistent bad management could possibly destroy BSA, as of course it ultimately did. At that time the outrageously flamboyant Dockers were the company's best known representatives and we prospered.

My five years as an apprentice ran its appointed course through the service department, mechanical test, tool room, E section, heat treatment, Gold Star engine and machine build, and finally to the competition shop. Bill Nicholson, David Tye, Fred Rist and a host of other riders of the day were constantly passing through and adding to the stories and excitement of that small department. Successive competition managers added to the ever-growing list of victories and BSA chose well these guiding lights. Bert Perrigo, Dennis Hardwicke, and finally — and perhaps the most successful of them all — Brian Martin. Brian recognised before anyone else that horsepower was not the answer in off-road racing and anticipated the lightweight two-strokes by three years and provided four-stroke machines which were 50 and 60 lb lighter than our rivals! This certainly meant putting aside the Gold Stars but it ensured BSA of a dominance which was to spread through two decades, the last vestiges of which we still see today in the CCM and other specials. Now after ten years of two-stroke dominance the wheel has turned full circle and the Japanese are bringing out lightweight single-cylinder four-strokes. As I have long suspected and hoped, the four-stroke 'is not dead — only sleeping'.

But the competition department and its heads were not BSA. BSA was a great and diverse company and its downfall and mismanagement may be accurately pinpointed to those who took over after the departure of the Dockers. From then on the downward path was only arrested from time to time. One short period was full of hope; that was when Harry Sturgeon of the piercing blue eyes, briefly led the company to high profits and then tragically passed away at the height of his success. His policies and plans were imperfectly understood by those who followed and from then on the downward path was precipitous. By the late 1960s the Japanese threat was clearly perceived yet the ostrich syndrome took over upper management to such an extent that on returning from the US after a lecture tour and reporting that one complaint I had heard concerned oil leaks, I was bawled at by one of the managers that 'our engines do not leak and cannot leak because the finish is too good,' and that 'something happens to them on the Atlantic!'

Further, on submitting a comparison report on a Suzuki 6 against our 250 Barracuda which was unfavourable to our machine, I was called before another manager and told 'We have the Japs beaten for performance, quality and price, and next year we shall butcher them in the market place!' History, of course, paints a different picture. Managerial incompetence, lack of foresight, huge sums spent ludicrously and unfinished products finally dragged down a proud and great company. Thousands of workers and faithful craftsmen were turned out and the great edifice came crashing down.

Yet the human mind plays tricks and the bitterness of those last few months is now softened into nostalgic memories of that busy happy factory full of friends where I spent 20 years striving with them to make the whole thing work.

Will BSA ever rise again? I have occasionally been contacted by groups of American business men who have asked the same question — could it be done? Maybe, but as Bob Holliday so eloquently points out, Armoury Road is gone so the old 'Beesa' could never be truly at home again.

I think Bob has written a really fine volume. I thoroughly enjoyed reading it, and even learnt a great deal about a company for which I worked for 20 years! The book will, I am sure, be a great success, and I am pleased to be associated with it.

Duluth, Minnesota 1978   Jeff Smith MBE

BSA Story in brief

1861 The Birmingham Small Arms Company Limited formed to make guns by machinery at Small Heath.

1873 Name changed to Birmingham Small Arms & Metal Company. Adderley Park works acquired to make munitions.

1878 Production switched from weapons to components for the bicycle trade.

1880 Piled Arms trademark adopted and applied to BSA's first road vehicle, the Otto Dicycle.

1897 The company reverted to its original title.

1905 Experimental motor cycle made with a foreign engine.

1910 First wholly BSA-made motor cycle marketed, a 3½ hp single-cylinder belt-driver. Acquisition of the Daimler motor car concern.

1913 First race win by a BSA, averaging over 60 mph at Brooklands track. Thirteen BSAs in the IoM TT race.

1914 Single-cylinder 4½ hp (557 cc) all-chain model with patent three-speed gear. BSA produced their own sidecars. Six out of eight BSAs finished in the TT. Concentration on war work — guns, motor cycles and cycles.

1916 Government stopped sales of civilian vehicles.

1918 BSA work force at the end of the Great War was 13,000 employees. Factory space trebled.

1919 Formation of BSA Cycles Ltd to make motor cycles and cycles. First V-twin Model E 6-7 hp exhibited at Olympia.

1920 Works-entered BSA riders won the Scottish Six Days Trial team prize.

1921 All five BSA works riders gained 'Scottish' gold medals. Six hush-hush ohv machines with knife-edge rockers in the TT; none finished. Commander Godfrey Herbert, DSO, succeeded Charles Hyde as BSA Cycles managing director.

1922 V-twin model uprated to 8 hp (986 cc). H. S. Perrey joined the company as assistant to chief engineer F. W. Hulse.

1923 Side-valve sports single-cylinder models introduced, built at the BSA Redditch works, formerly the Eadie Manufacturing Company.

1924 'Round-tank' 249 cc Model B two-speed side-valver created a sensation at under £40. Also introduced was BSA's first ohv roadster, a 350 cc vertical single. Multi-model hill-climbing demonstrations on Screw Hill and Snowdon staged by Harry Perrey.

1925 Improved ohv 350 cc Super Sports model arrived.

1926 With its inclined cylinder, the ohv 493 cc 'Sloper' hit the headlines. Sixty climbs of Bwlch-y-Groes with a 350 cc sidecar outfit won the Maudes Trophy. A. E. Perrigo joined the competitions department.

1927 B. H. Cathrick and J. P. Castley began a world tour with two 8 hp sidecar outfits, covering 25,000 land miles in 19 months.

1928 First two-stroke, 174 cc Model A, marketed. Redditch factory sold and all production transferred to Small Heath.

1929 BSA three-wheeler launched with air-cooled, ohv V-twin engine. Bert Perrigo (349 BSA) solo winner of the first British Experts Trial.

1930 Programme listed 12 motor cycles and three types of three-wheeler.

1931 Blue Star 350 cc ohv sports machines with four-speed gearboxes made their bow.

1932 Victory Trial won by Perrigo; team prize by BSA, all with Blue Stars.

1933 Water-cooled, four-cylinder three-wheelers introduced. Fluid-flywheel motor cycle shown at Olympia.

1934 Advertising manager J. W. Bryan appointed to BSA Cycles board. Fred Povey and Harold Flook solo and sidecar British Experts, each repeating previous successes, Flook for the third time.

1935 Celebrating King George V's Silver Jubilee, a new range of BSAs — Empire Stars — were show-stoppers in a display of 18 different models.

1936 Ace-designer Valentine Page, moved from Ariel to BSA, revamped the range, especially the Empire Stars.

1937 Riding a Page-type Empire Star, Walter Handley won a BMCRC 'gold star' for a lap of the Brooklands track at 107.57 mph. 500 cc Model M24 Gold Star introduced at first-ever Earls Court Show.

1938 BSA won another Maudes Trophy long-distance test with a solo Empire Star and an M21 combination.

1939 Back to war work, with the group, led by chief executive James Leek, achieving stupendous production of arms, munitions, and vehicles including M20 motor cycles and paratroop cycles.

1944 Ariel Motors Ltd acquired by BSA.

1945 A four-model post-war range included a new 348 cc ohv model, the long-popular B31 with telescopic front fork.

1946 Sunbeam ohc vertical twin arrived, made at Redditch wartime shadow factory. Small

Heath produced the 495 cc Model A7 twin. Fred Rist and Bill Nicholson joined the competitions staff.

1947 ZB-type Gold Stars were raced in the first IoM Clubman's TT.

1948 BSA's most successful two-stroke, the Bantam, began its long reign.

1949 The 646 cc A10 Golden Flash joined the range. Harold Clark (350 Gold Star) won the Junior Clubman's TT.

1950 John Draper, Basil Hall and John Avery joined the competitions squad. Harold Tozer was the first winner of the ACU Sidecar Trials Drivers Star.

1951 Jack Sangster sold the Triumph Engineering Company to BSA for £2½m, becoming a group director.

1952 Brian Martin, a comp shop member, won the Victory Trial. Gene Thiessen broke world's records with A7 and A10 twins on Bonneville Salt Flats. Another Maudes Trophy award for a round-Europe team ride that took in the International Six Days Trial.

1953 BSA Cycles Ltd, and BSA Motor Cycles Ltd formed as separate companies. Jeffrey Smith, aged 17, started his 20-year spell as a BSA competitions star.

1954 Star Twins first and second in the 200-mile race on Daytona Beach.

1955 Herbert Hopwood appointed chief engineer at Small Heath. Dandy 70 and Beesa scooters shown at Earls Court.

1956 Parent board chairman Sir Bernard Docker replaced by Jack Sangster. Edward Turner succeeded retiring James Leek as chief executive. BSA Cycles Ltd sold to Raleigh Industries. On Gold Stars, Bernard Codd 'doubled' the last Clubman's TT.

1957 Group profits showed an increase to £2.1m from £1.6m.

1958 New 250 cc C15 Star design became the basis for many successful derivatives. Production of Sunbeam twins and BSA sidecars ceased. BSA/Triumph Sunbeam and Tigress scooters launched.

1959 Arthur Lampkin won the Scrambles Drivers Star contest.

1960 Eric Turner joined the board as group chief executive.

1961 BSA's centenary. Jack Sangster retired, Eric Turner succeeding as chairman. Record profit of nearly £3½m.

1962 Unit-construction A50 and A65 twins, and Beagle lightweight, introduced. Chris Vincent won BSA's only International TT with a 500 cc twin sidecar outfit.

1963 Ariel Motors transferred to Small Heath. Harry Sturgeon succeeded Edward Turner as managing director.

1964 Victor B41 441 cc models developed from earlier 420 cc type.

1966 Edward Turner retired from the parent board.

1967 BSA granted Queen's Award for Industry. Harry Sturgeon died, being succeeded by Lionel Jofeh. Umberslade Hall research centre set up.

1968 BSA again granted the Queen's Award. Three-cylinder 750 cc Rocket Three model announced.

1969 Rocket Threes first and second in Thruxton endurance grand prix.

1970 Jeff Smith became a Member of the British Empire.

1971 BSA group lost over £8m. Eric Turner resigned. Lord Shawcross became chairman. Competitions department closed.

1972 Group lost a further £3m.

1973 BSA group virtually bankrupt. Absorbed by Norton Villiers Triumph with capital subscribed by Manganese Bronze Holdings and the government. Extinction of the Piled Arms marque.

1974 Plans for production of Triumph engines at Small Heath ran into trouble.

1975 Buildings and land on Armoury Road site sold to Birmingham Corporation.

1976 Complete demolition of the original office-factory building.

1977 Death of Jack Sangster, aged 80. Rocket Threes won IoM Formula One TT team prize, headed by Malcolm Lucas, placed fifth on the first British machine to finish.

Chapter 1

Much genius in Bermingham

'Now thrive the armourers' — *Henry V*

If King William III (remember him — William and Mary, 1689-1694?) hadn't complained that guns and swords were not procurable in England and had to be bought 'at great expense and greater difficulty' from Holland, the initials BSA might never have graced the sides of a motor-cycle tank.

His Majesty's moan happened to be heard by one of the Members of Parliament for Warwick-shire, Sir Richard Newdegate, who was quick to remark on behalf of his constituents that 'much genius resides in Warwickshire', where Birmingham smiths were 'well able to answer the royal wishes'. The upshot was a trial order from the Crown in 1689 which, being satisfactorily executed, led to a contract between Their Majesties' Office of Ordnance and five of Birmingham's principal gunsmiths who, along with other master craftsmen, undertook to supply 200 Snaphance muskets monthly, 'at 17 shillings per piece, ready money'.

Being a Dutchman, and only just enthroned, William probably had not realised when he made his complaint that for more than a century the Midlands had been England's centre for metal working, Black Country 'sea coal' having caused the transference of the craft from the charcoal-burning, ore-smelting smithies of the Kent and Sussex Weald. Way back in 1538 an itinerant churchman, John Leland, had written in his journal: 'I came to a praty street or ever I entered Bermingham, as I remember it called Dirty [Deritend] there being many smiths in the towne, that use to make knives and all manner of cutting tools, and many lorimers that make bittes, and a great many naylours, so that a great part of the towne is maintained by smiths, who have their iron and sea-coal out of Staffordshire'.

To the production of knives, daggers, swords and other cutting tools, Birmingham's artisans had, following the increasing use of gunpowder, added the manufacture of firearms, making not only complete weapons but also furnishing barrels and locks to gunmakers in other parts of the realm. A 17th-century English visitor to Milan, commenting on the 'fine works of steel there', nevertheless remarked that 'they could be had better and cheaper in Birmingham'.

So there were no problems for the Warwickshire smiths when their MP's commendation brought them their initial government contract, and for 150 years a system of co-operative working by the Birmingham trade continued and developed into a prodigious industry. Vast quantities of firearms were made and supplied not only to British, but also foreign armies. When Waterloo ended the Napoleonic wars some 7,000 workers were turning out weapons at the rate of half a million a year.

Bonaparte's final defeat brought a lull in the military arms trade but the Birmingham producers were kept going by London, Liverpool and Bristol merchants who found an eager market for cheap guns among the natives of Africa, who paid for their muzzle-loaders with gold, spices and ivory — white and black.

Big government contracts returned to the Midlands during the war in the Crimea and in 18 months 150,000 Brummagem rifles were supplied to the British forces, as against 75,000 bought by the War Department from all other sources at home and abroad. All the weapons were hand made, and it was at this period that two important factors emerged to warn the Warwickshire gun makers that their community system of contracting was in danger of extinction. Manufacture by machinery was one; the other was the establishment of a Government arms factory at Enfield, in Middlesex. By 1855 this factory was fully mechanised and, when the Crimean War ended in 1856, it had reached an output of over 2,000 rifles and carbines a week. No matter how vociferously the Birmingham trade protested the superiority of hand-made guns, orders fell alarmingly. The old arrangement of sharing out contracts among a number of relatively small workshops had to end for it was clearly uneconomical to equip each of the individual smithies with expensive machinery that, in order to pay for itself, needed large, uninterrupted, long-term orders, not to mention the further capital outlay required for premises to house the machines and for the motive power to operate them.

Concentration, rather than deployment, of work was the only practical way to combat competition from Enfield, and in June 1861 leading members of the Birmingham Small Arms Association met together to form the Birmingham Small Arms Company Limited, with an initial capital of £24,500 and the resolve to manufacture guns by machinery.

The first act of the newly formed company was to buy a 25-acre site at Small Heath, on the south-east side of the city. They paid £300 an acre and at a cost of £17,500 built the office and factory edifice that for over 100 years remained the centrepoint of an increasingly widespread industrial empire — The BSA*.

It was a typical late-Victorian, red-brick structure, with no more architectural inspiration than that of an infirmary, prison or superior workhouse. In the form of a hollow square, the building was mainly on two floors with three-storey blocks in the centre of the façade and at each corner. Surrounding a central courtyard were the offices, engineering and woodworking shops, foundry and power house, the whole complex being overtopped by a tall, incessantly smoking chimney. On one side of the site, sidings connected with the Great Western Railway main line and round the back curved a section of the Grand Union canal system.

From its 'front door' the company constructed a half-mile-long private road — Armoury Road — to link with Golden Hillock Road, an important thoroughfare joining the Coventry road to the east of the city with the Warwick and Stratford roads in the south. It was in this neighbourhood — Small Heath, Sparkbrook, Greet, Digbeth and Deritend (the 'Dirty End' of John Leland's day) — that many of the original members of the BSA consortium had had their places of work and later it saw the beginnings of some of the city's pioneer cycle and motor-cycle firms — James, Norton, Calthorpe, Watsonian sidecars and Humphries and Dawes of OK fame, being among the best remembered.

Mention of such names takes my memory back over half a century to my first impression of the Midlands two-wheeler industry, gained when, in 1928, I made my initial acquaintance with the area as *Motor Cycling's* resident representative. In those days, so it seemed to me, the 'bike trade' was divided into two distinct classes. On the one hand there were the dozens of small but well-known and well-established

firms, tucked away in hard-to-find sidestreets, sometimes actually making their own engines, but more often relying entirely on proprietary units and bought-out components. Apart from frame brazing, wheel building and enamelling, they were really nothing else but assemblers. The 'gaffer' had a reasonably sized office, with a desk and an armchair, but the works manager, the sales chief and the rest of the business staff were generally to be found in cramped little cubbyholes, working on hard stools at wooden benches. From the back of the premises came the heat and smell of the brazing hearths and the paint baths.

At the other end of the scale were the solidly imposing, purpose-built citadels of the industry's giants — Royal Enfield at Redditch, New Hudson in the city centre, Components Ltd (the Ariel headquarters) in Selly Oak, Villiers, Sunbeam and AJS in Wolverhampton, Raleigh in Nottingham, and Triumph, Humber and Rudge-Whitworth in Coventry. I particularly recall the solemn stateliness of aspect they presented to the visitor. Having passed the suspicious scrutiny of the janitor in his vestibule sentry-box, one usually climbed a sweeping flight of stairs to reach the management on the upper floor. Here was a portrait gallery of bearded founders and past chairmen, a wealth of solid mahogany or dark oak, stuffed-leather furniture and ponderous inkstands — not a sliver of veneer or a flash of chrome in sight.

Thus it was at Small Heath when I first passed down Armoury Road 50 years ago. Although gun-making was then only a small part of BSA activity, the place still preserved the forbidding atmosphere of an ordnance factory accustomed to high-level dealing with Ministries and war departments on an international scale. Whereas at, for example, the Ariel works, the commissionaire cheerily greeted the visitor with the news that 'Mr Davies is in his office — go right ahead', at Small Heath there were iron gates in Armoury Road and a caller had to satisfy the security guards as to his identity and nature of business. Even then he might have to wait while his credentials were checked and somebody from the office block came to conduct him to the department or person he wished to contact.

*   *   *

*Prefixing the name of a company with the definite article has long been a Midlands custom. In and around Birmingham one works, not at Wolseley Motors or Morris Engines, but at The Wolseley or The Morris.

The first two years in the life of the Birmingham Small Arms Company were not notable for lively progress.

Administration was by a committee consisting of all the shareholders, a form of control notoriously inefficient and time-wasting. However, in September 1863, at an extraordinary general meeting, a board of directors was elected, with Mr J. D. Goodman as chairman and Mr J. F. Swinburn vice-chairman; there were seven other members and it seems that all these gentlemen were well chosen, since between them they gave the company many years of wise and loyal service.

Mr Goodman himself remained chairman until his death in 1900, and during his 37 years in office he skilfully guided BSA affairs through good times and bad. And some of them were very bad, for the Government tended more and more to rely on its Enfield arms factory and only in periods of national crisis was Small Heath called upon to help out. Fortunately — if that is the right word — crises seemed to crop up in the nick of time and, if there were no orders from Whitehall, Continental quarrels like the Austro-Prussian and the Franco-Prussian wars were good for business. By 1868 BSA had become the largest private arms company in Europe and the factory was working to full capacity.

In 1873 came an order from the Prussian Government for 40,000,000 cartridge cases. To execute this, the company reorganised itself by going into voluntary liquidation and selling its assets to a new concern, the Birmingham Small Arms and Metal Company, and a new factory at nearby Adderley Park was set up to produce ammunition. Not until 24 years later, in 1897, did the firm revert to its original title, when the Adderley Park business was sold to the Nobel Dynamite Trust, which in due course became Imperial Chemical Industries.

Chapter 2

Piled Arms and pedalling legs

'Round went the wheels' — *John Gilpin*

It was in 1880 that BSA adopted their celebrated trademark, the sign of the Piled Arms, representing the infantryman's traditional method of stacking guns in pyramid formation. But it was piling of another kind — stockpiling, in fact — that had, a couple of years earlier, caused an upheaval at Small Heath. Early in 1878 the British Government declared that for the next 12 months it would not be issuing any armament or munitions contracts. Furthermore, it had decided to sell off a stock of 100,000 rifles which, it said, were obsolete, Out of date they might have been, but they were perfectly good, brand-new weapons and, at an auction held at Weedon, in Northants, the whole lot were snapped up in a few minutes by a horde of foreign buyers.

Knowledge that Britain then stood in immediate danger of involvement in a war between Russia and Turkey, together with the fact that the auction had added only some £15,000 to Treasury funds, aroused a storm of public indignation, which ultimately brought about a prohibition of sales of Government arms. Henceforth, obsolete weapons had to be broken up for scrap.

However, that was no help to BSA, who were not only deprived of British contracts but had seen potential foreign orders disappear as European belligerents equipped themselves from the Weedon auction at knockdown prices. Immediately the factory went on to half-time working, and four months later it was shut down completely, remaining closed for a full year.

Drastic as this measure was, it had a beneficial outcome, for it compelled the directors to look around for some other form of employment for their men and machinery, less dependent on War Office whims, competition with the Enfield plant and spasmodic outbreaks of Continental hostilities.

In nearby Coventry, Joseph Starley had fathered the bicycle, and the bicycle boom was beginning to burgeon. Already names like Rover, Humber, Rudge and Singer were household words and scores of makers were seeking their shares of the bonanza. Not so many, however, were equipped to construct complete machines and there was a large demand for cycle parts — frame lugs and brackets, wheel rims, hubs, brakes, crank and pedal assemblies, chains, tyres and saddles. For the production of small castings and forgings, presswork and general light engineering jobs, the BSA workshops were splendidly suited and, when the factory re-opened in the autumn of 1879 to fulfil a relatively small Government order for rifles, a proportion of the plant capacity was converted to the manufacture of fittings and parts for the cycle trade.

Making bicycle bits and pieces for other people was one thing; to design and launch a complete machine of their own construction was felt by the BSA board to be an undertaking rather beyond the capabilities of their technicians who, skilled though they were in the arts and crafts of armaments, had practically no experience that would enable them to contest the already crowded market for bicycles.

Mr Goodman and his colleagues thought they had found an alternative when an inventor, Mr E. C. F. Otto, offered them the rights to make an entirely new kind of cycle which he had patented. Its novelty lay in the fact that, instead of having the wheels disposed in single-track form, they were arranged on each side of the rider's seat, were driven by a kind of treadle and steered by a pair of upright handles. The machine was, in fact, a tricycle, for stability was achieved by means of a small wheel trailing at the end of a down-curved rear member, after the fashion of a 'penny-farthing'.

Mr Otto was invited to bring his Dicycle, as he called it, to a directors' meeting, and his method of demonstrating it was to ride it up and down the boardroom table, after which he pedalled down the stairs and into Armoury Road, disappearing towards Birmingham at what one elderly director described as a 'reckless pace'.

The gaffers must have been impressed, for they decided to build 200 machines to Otto's design and so, in 1880, the sign of the Piled Arms made its entry into the world of wheels. And it was not long before Small Heath was making conventional bicycles and tricycles, both to its own designs and to those of other firms, who put their individual trademarks on the headstocks and sold the machines through their own resources.

Profitable though it was, the cycle section of BSA's business was still regarded as only a sideline to the main task of gun production and when, in 1888, the War Office decided to equip the British Army with a new type of rifle, the Lee-Metford, Small Heath was ordered to produce these weapons at the rate of 1,200 a week. The magnitude of the contract called for the full capacity of the works and with regret — for over a span of eight years BSA bikes and trikes had become extremely popular — the directors agreed to abandon cycle building.

Four years were to pass before BSA came back to bicycles, and when they did it was not as constructors of complete machines, but in their old role as suppliers of components to an industry that had grown to fantastic proportions. Cycling had become a world-wide pastime and sport, epitomised by the immortal Daisy Bell and her bicycle made for two.

To cope with the demand, the Adderley Park munitions plant was re-equipped to make cycle components; to handle the repetition work, women, for the first time, were employed, and a night shift was introduced. By 1895 orders worth over £4,500 a week were coming in and Armoury Road was built up on one side with terrace houses for BSA work people and on the other side with multi-storey workshops that contained the latest automatic machinery designed for mass production.

By this time motor cars, mostly imported, were becoming popular in Britain, and the BSA machine shops were ideally equipped for the construction of such vehicles. The company did, indeed, carry out an order for a small quantity of internal combustion engines but, before there was time to develop this obviously promising line of business, the Boer War was boiling up and the War Office was sending out panic telegrams calling for rifles, and yet more rifles. At BSA, cycle work went overboard and the whole organisation, rapidly expanding with new buildings, was once again concentrated on small arms, to such an extent that when the South African campaign closed, the company was producing 2,500 rifles a week.

And then, what? As had so frequently happened before, the British Government, its urgent needs fulfilled, sat back and left the private industry contractors to fend for themselves. Moreover, officialdom appeared completely to ignore the intrusion of Germany into tradition-ally British fields of commerce. Unable to find enough orders, and facing all kinds of fierce, often unscrupulous, Teutonic competition, many of the British engineering companies that had devoted themselves solely to war work, went out of business, and that fate might have overtaken BSA had the company not been able to fall back on its capacity for cycle making.

The Boer War had not diminished the popularity of the bicycle and soon Small Heath had not only resumed their components trade but, in 1908, after a lapse of 20 years, the initials BSA again appeared on machines wholly constructed in the firm's workshops. An export department was set up and the Piled Arms guarantee of good workmanship spread to the Continent where, in France and Belgium, a proud owner would refer to his mount as a *Trois Fusils*.

The company's earlier brief experience with petrol engines had been followed, in 1905, by a one-off experiment consisting of a standard-type bicycle built from BSA parts and having a small proprietary engine clipped, after the manner of the period, to the front down-tube. The front fork was strutted for extra strength and a fuel tank hung from the top rail. A much-faded photograph of this machine shows an engine looking very like a French-made Clement or a Belgian Minerva, both being units in general use at the time. James L. Norton's first motor cycle had a Clement engine and the great Triumph marque was founded on Minervas.

BSA's first tentative attempt to make a motor cycle remained only as a prototype, and five more years passed before the company went seriously into the powered two-wheeler industry which, by 1910, had long outgrown its teething troubles and was expanding on a reputation for providing an economical and reliable means of travel.

It is probable that the BSA motor cycle would have been followed by a BSA car had the company not, at the same time, been negotiating the acquisition of the Daimler Motor Company, Britain's first motor manufactory, established in Coventry in 1896. At all events, with feet firmly planted in the pedalling world, an assured outlet through its cycle distributors for a well-made motor cycle, and an already famous motor marque to feed its vast maw of machinery, the Birmingham Small Arms Company set aside the arts of war and turned diligently to the exciting and fast-growing field of road transport.

Chapter 3

Right first time

'In truth, he was a noble steed' — *Lord Byron*

Although comparatively late in entering the motor-cycle market, BSA's first offering to the riding public was, right from the start, a good 'un, and *Motor Cycling,* describing the new-comer for 1911, said: '. . . the BSA is by no means a potterer. What astonishes us is that such an excellent example of the touring motor bicycle should have been evolved by a concern practically at the first attempt.'

It was, in fact, the outcome of a lengthy and secret period of preparation and, until the technical journals published details in their 1910 Olympia Show numbers, very few people outside the trade had any inkling of the Small Heath project. Indeed, the new models were not even made at Small Heath, but in a factory at Lodge Road, Redditch, formerly the Eadie Manufacturing Company which had been absorbed in 1908 and which had produced the Eadie coaster hub — 'back-pedalling brake' — for bicycles.

It was Albert Eadie, together with another free-wheel inventor, Charles A. Hyde, and an engine designer, F. E. Baker, who converted the Redditch premises to motor-cycle making and prepared the specification of the first machines to carry BSA's green and yellow livery on to British roads. Frank Baker, a pioneer Tourist Trophy race rider, had considerable motor-cycle experience and later produced the famous Precision engines and built machines carrying his own surname. Charles Hyde, too, was a practical motor cyclist for, before transferring to BSA, he had been works manager at the James Cycle Company which had been making motor bicycles since 1902. Albert Eadie joined the BSA board and continued to be a director until the mid-1920s.

At first glance the new 3½ hp, 499 cc (85 × 88 mm) BSA motor cycle seemed to be a pretty conventional job, but it had some unusual features, particularly, as might be expected from transmission specialists such as Eadie and Hyde, in the driving gear, Also, it had a front fork that must have been one of the earliest examples of two-way springing. The following description is reproduced, with only slight editing, from a 'What the Show will Reveal' feature that appeared in the October 25, 1910 issue of *Motor*

Cycling:

THE NEW BSA MOTOR-BICYCLE. A 3½ hp MACHINE ON STANDARD LINES WITH SEVERAL NOTABLE IMPROVEMENTS.

On Wednesday last we were privileged to inspect the new 3½ hp single-cylinder BSA motor-bicycle, which has been tested and considered in detail for the past 12 months. The machine is made at the Redditch works of the Birmingham Small Arms Co, and will sell for £50 or £56 10s when fitted with the company's patent cone clutch in the rear hub. The latter fitment has not yet been patented and the only details we can give at present are that it is operated by a lever from the left footrest, and that the belt rim is spoked independently of the wheel. We rode the machine and found the cone clutch extraordinarily sweet in action as the drive was taken up.

The standard pedal-fitted model follows well accepted lines. [Auxiliary cycle-type pedalling gear was generally used with single-speed, direct-belt drive up to World War I.] The machine has a chain-driven Bosch magneto placed in front of the engine, with the B & B carburettor feeding mixture through a mechanically operated inlet valve.

Perhaps it will be wise to describe the engine first. The valves are situated side by side, and the exhaust tappet is adjustable by means of a threaded head, which is locked by another nut to the tappet stem. Round the heads of both the inlet and exhaust tappets are fitted dust caps, which come down over the tops of the tappet guides and prevent the egress of oil or the intrusion of dust. Another feature whereby the timing gear is made oiltight is the fitting of dustcaps over the ends of the timing shafts. These caps are cast integral with the aluminium cover, and are very neat. Quite light springs are fitted to the one-piece valves, which are made of nickel steel.

The cylinder head is provided with vertical flanges cast parallel with the direction of travel, whilst in the centre there is the compression tap. Large valve pockets, ball-bearing mainshafts, and a low compression space are three features of the engine, whilst a particularly fine piece of work is the piston. This is domed, with two step-cut rings above the gudgeon pin and an oil grove at the bottom. The way the gudgeon pin is held in position is very clever. At one end of the pin is cut a groove. There is also a slight groove in one of the bosses of the piston. A piece of spring wire is placed around the groove on the gudgeon pin, and the latter is then gently tapped up along the taper in the bosses. As soon as the spring registers with the groove in the inside of the boss it expands, and then locks the pin in the piston. A smart tap in the reverse direction suffices to loosen the pin again.

The most remarkable departure from standard practice is the magneto box. This is made of aluminium, and is fixed firmly to a platform. Sliding doors give access to the contact breaker and high-tension terminal sides of the magneto. The doors are provided with knobs to facilitate opening, and are locked by milled-headed screws. The high-tension wire emerges from the box via a watertight fibre guide hole. A double stay from the front down-tube supports the bracket of the box. The rubber-faced footrests pass through the magneto chain drive, and it is worth noting that the brake pedal is mounted separately from the footrests. On the brake pedal is cast a guide to prevent the inside of the foot slipping away when applying the brake shoe. The latter is fitted above the rear chain stay, and in this position is more powerful than if mounted underneath.

An excellent system of mudguards is fitted to the front wheel. In addition to side flaps, there is an extra splasher guard extending almost parallel to the ground. By means of two flat pieces of spring-steel, the splasher is kept in position, although it can give upwards should it encounter any very serious obstacle in the road, such as a brick [!]

The spring fork is also constructed on novel lines. The girders are connected to the steering head by four cross links in the ordinary way, but between the outer ends of the lower pair of links is mounted an extension piece carrying two springs — the lower and larger being in compression and the smaller and higher one in tension. This combination of springs, and also the angle at which they are set, should absorb much of the alleged bogy of motor-cycling vibration. The handlebars are provided with horn undergrips for the hands, and a lamp bracket is made in one with the bar.

The rear portion of the machine is designed on well-tried lines, with luggage-carrier and two toolboxes set athwart it, a stand, and last, but not least, the new BSA patent free wheel hub. The special feature of this device is that it is impossible for the free wheel to become clogged with water or mud, as it is entirely protected, and situated inside the covering plate. The pedals themselves are fastened to the cranks by a double locking arrangement, so that there should be no possibility of their coming adrift.

The finish of the tank is distinctive without being vulgar, and special care has been taken to prevent oil and petrol from exuding from their various compartments. With this object in view, the oil pump and filler cap fit down a circular recess fitted into their respective openings. The idea of these guides is to catch any oil that may emerge from the tank at any time. Arrangements are made for ventilating the tanks.

The adjustable pulley can be altered by hand alone. On the boss, which is part of the inside flange, is fitted a key. This corresponds with a keyway cut in the outer flange, which thus can slide up and down the boss and varies the gear. The outer face of the sliding flange is drilled with a number of holes. Screwing on the boss is a milled locking ring, which has on its inner face a projecting knob. The locknut is screwed up until the desired position is reached, when the outer flange is slid outwards until one of the holes engages with the knob and locks the whole pulley solid. The pressure of the belt also helps in this. The cut-out is another simple fitment. It is operated by the foot and brings into action a single slit in the end of the silencer.

We were privileged to have a short run on the machine, and we may say at once that the three things that impressed us most were the slow running, the absence of engine vibration at low speed, and the great silence of the machine at moderate speed. We turned the machine round in an ordinary road without any difficulty, and this with a standard gear. Probably the low compression accounts for the extraordinary smoothness of running and absence of vibration, while the silencer is responsible for the ease and tranquillity of the machine at touring speeds. The engine is reported by those who have ridden it to have climbed such hills as Birdlip and Sunrising with ease after a long run, whilst other reports that we have received from riders on the road state that the BSA is by no means a potterer . . . The workmanship is worthy of the BSA reputation, and the short spin already referred to has made us long for a more intimate acquaintance with the engine which we hope, by courtesy of the company, to soon have the opportunity of gratifying.

The hoped-for courtesy was duly extended, and a fortnight later *Motor Cycling's* editor, W. G. McMinnies, was able to record his impressions of '120 Miles of Mud-plugging on a BSA'. As a 'road test' this account does not stand up to the modern style of lucid analysis (any more than did the technical description), but as a piece of candid personal writing it is delightfully evocative of the pleasures and perils of motor-cycling journalism in those leisurely early days. Now read on . . .

When it is pouring with rain, and there is a biting north-west wind blowing, motor cycling is not an enviable pastime, and yet, when our representative left Birmingham last week on one of the new 3½ hp BSA motor bicycles, he was quite happy, for it might have been much worse. Cutting across the Moseley Road from the BSA works, he was soon splashing along over flooded roads, and it was lucky the machine was shod with rubber non-skids.

The engine exhibited plenty of flexibility, and was particularly silent, but when the cut-out was opened it had an extraordinarily healthy bark. Somewhere on the outskirts of Birmingham, Dunlop patches and valve tubing were bought as there were none in the kit, a surprise puncture having found this out. The Alcester road was then taken for about a dozen miles, and then a sharp turn down a by-lane at Redditch, which could be seen nestling in the distance in a cloud of smoke. At the Unicorn Hotel, the waders and umbrella coat removed, a hasty lunch was disposed of.

It was 4.15 on a November afternoon when a start was made again for London — the wind had dried out the roads and the sun shone. Alcester was soon passed, and then the Stratford road was taken, winding through a glorious district, still decked in much of its summer charms. Gradually the night drew on, and when the machine sped through Stratford it was nearly five. A few miles further on a Little Briton car hove in sight, the owner being Mr John Gibson, the Trump motor bicyclist. He was introduced to the BSA, and after a few words the motorists parted. The long hill out of Long Compton was taken in grand style in the semi-darkness and as, when nearing Chipping Norton, a cart nearly collided with the machine, it was thought better to stop the night at the 'White Hart'.

Tea and eggs followed, and half an hour in the evening was spent tightening the belt by putting up the hand adjustable pulley. A smaller jet was also inserted, as the engine was taking all air and one quarter throttle. Next morning, at 7.45 am, a start was made for London. The icy air chilled the rider's face to the bone, and speed had to be reduced. Near Enstone the machine stopped, and a cursory examination showed petrol pouring from the carburettor, the float cover of which had come undone. This did not cause much delay, and it was 8.30 as the BSA rolled through Bicester. Here the old Quarterly Trials route was taken, and a short stop was made to inspect the oil pump, as it was not quite certain whether oil was reaching the engine. It was found to be working properly. At Berkhamsted petrol was taken aboard, and soon afterwards E. A. Colliver and his Triumph (a combination well known in the Herts County AC) were passed. Then a gallant little 3½ hp Peugeot and sidecar were

overhauled, but the series of 10-mile speed limits after Watford reduced speed considerably. The long line of trams down the Edgware Road, which was in an abominable condition, caused many qualms to our representative, who arrived at *Motor Cycling* offices in Rosebery Avenue, London, EC, about ten minutes past eleven in pouring rain.

The BSA ran splendidly, and the engine is one of the very finest touring machines on the road. The crankcase had not exuded any oil from the timing gear, so that the oil caps on the tappets must be very efficient.

W.G. McM

A picture accompanying the article shows the travel-worn rider-writer astride the BSA outside his journal's London offices, having just completed his 120-mile journey in the best part of a day and a half. Since the machine carried lighting equipment, one might wonder why it was 'thought better' to spend the night at Chipping Norton, but those acquainted with Gordon McMinnies will find nothing surprising about that. Never a desk-bound journalist, he was a keen competitor; he raced at Brooklands and in the Isle of Man, and drove his Morgan three-wheeler, 'Jabberwock', to victory in a French Grand Prix. But he also enjoyed the creature comforts and later in life became one of the best-known compilers of 'good food guides for motorists'. His references in the foregoing mud-plug story to a 'hasty lunch' that extended to 4.15 pm, followed by tea and eggs at Chipping Norton's comfortable 'White Hart', are an early revelation of his conviction that, if travel broadens the mind, it also stimulates the taste buds.

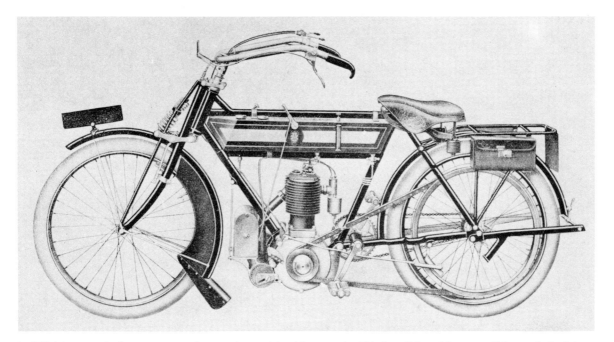

1: *BSA entered the motor-cycle market with this sturdy 3½ hp (85 x 88 mm, 499 cc) belt-driven machine, displayed at the 1910 Olympia Show. With an unusual, double-acting spring fork, it was constructed almost entirely from BSA-made components and was produced from the company's Redditch factory.*

2: *This earliest known photograph of BSA's Small Heath headquarters was taken about 1866, some five years after the founding of the company. The surrounding green fields were later built over, but in 1977 the site was once again an open space, bulldozers having razed the original structure.*

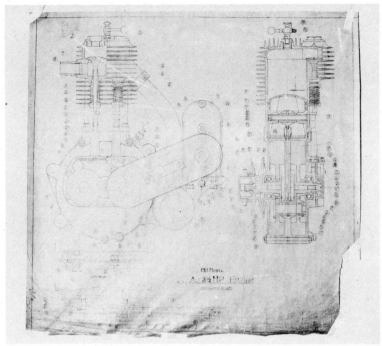

3: *Tattered, but still decipherable, is the general arrangement drawing, finely executed in Indian ink on linen, of BSA's first motor-cycle engine. After over 65 years in storage, it was photographed specially for this book. Note the detail of the patent variable engine-shaft pulley.*

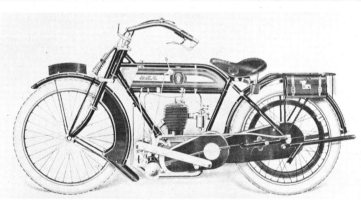

4: *With barely two years' experience of motor-cycle making, BSA were thoroughly up to date with their 1913 Model H, featuring enclosed all-chain drive, a pedal-operated two-speed hub gear and an own-make double-barrelled carburettor. It cost £60.*

5: *The original caption to this Great War picture read: 'Dispatch riders with BSA motor cycles pass a message to an Allied comrade with a more conventional means of transport.' Their 3½ hp machines had three-speed countershaft gearboxes.*

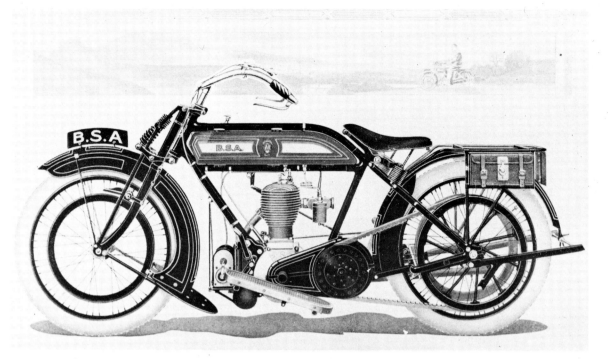

6: *Sales of civilian motor cycles were stopped by the government in 1916, by which time BSA had a 4¼ hp (557 cc) three-speed Model K that became immensely popular for both solo and sidecar use in the 1920s. Belt-rim brakes were fitted fore and aft, two on the rear wheel, with its tangentially spoked pulley.*

7: *Progenitor of BSA's long line of side-valve V-twins was the 1920 Model E, a 6-7 hp (770 cc) all-chain three-speeder whose solid construction won it a global reputation for reliable hard slogging.*

8: *Just out of the army, BSA's future competitions manager, Harry Perrey, straddles a 1920 3½ hp TT model, with a dropped frame, curvaceous handlebars and direct-belt drive. The push-pull, twin-springs front fork was still in use.*

9: *Harry Perrey's successes in competitions were mainly gained with sidecars, and this heavyweight outfit had a sprung third axle and a spare wheel. An Easting windscreen was fitted and Mr Easting stands proudly on the left.*

10: *Here is a scene that will recall memories for veteran Midlands trialsmen — a timecheck at the foot of Weatheroak Hill, near Alvechurch. Adjacent were two other notorious sections, Swans Lane and Icknield Street, and the Coach and Horses inn lurks handily in the background.*

11: *(Above) Carrying BSA's green and yellow racing colours, A. E. Taylor displays his 1921 Senior TT mount. Unlubricated ohv gear and finless cylinder heads caused difficulties not helped by erratic steering. Note the strapped-up saddle spring, and improvised kneegrips.*

12: *(Above right) A knife-edge rocker and valve-spring cap are all that remain of Bert Taylor's 1921 TT-racing BSA.*

13: *(Right) Another memory of BSA's ill-starred 1921 TT venture is this shot of Albert Wood, who raced in place of practice-injured Gus Kuhn. Today, he lives in Paignton, Devon, and his race teamster Bert Taylor (holding the front wheel) is a West Midlands garage proprietor.*

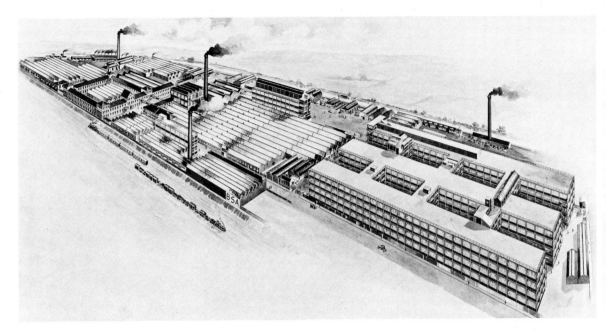

14: *Used to illustrate the 1921 BSA catalogue, this bird's-eye view shows how the Small Heath plant had grown around the original premises (top left). The four-storey complex in the right foreground was the New Building, erected during the Great War.*

15: *The famous 986 cc 'Beesa combo' in all its stately majesty, as it appeared in 1922. Most of it made in BSA workshops, it was sold as a complete outfit and the type provided dependable, inexpensive transport for many thousands of happy families through many years of production.*

16: *Harry Perrey, on an ohv 350, and George McLean, on a 'Round-tank' 250 sv prepare to tackle the rack-railway track to Snowdon's summit in May 1924. They each made the 3,500-foot-climb from Llanberis in around 30 minutes.*

17: *Through the snowdrifts and bumping over the railway sleepers, Harry Perrey urges his ohv 350 up the last stretches of the track with Snowdon's Summit Station beckoning to him from above.*

18: *Ted Thacker (foreground), George McLean (seated) and Jim Davis (atop the cairn) at the conclusion of BSA's Operation Snowdon. All three men made the ascent on 250 cc 'Round-tank' sv models.*

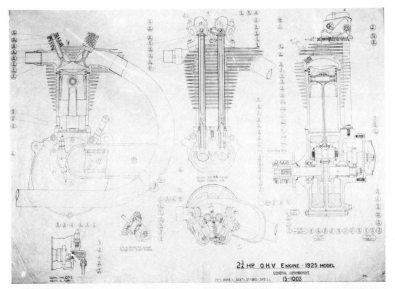

19: *A highly successful ohv single was the 2¾ hp (72 x 85.5 mm, 349 cc) Super Sports BSA which, in its early days, had duralumin pushrods. This photograph of the still-extant general arrangement drawing clearly reveals the main features of the 1925 engine.*

20: *The caption to this picture, taken in 1927, stressed that this was the correct and safe style for pillion riding! The girls, both BSA competition riders, were the Debenham sisters, Nancy and Betty, and the machine was the de luxe version of the 250 cc side-valver, at first famous for its round tank.*

21: *The cheers were for J. P. Castley and B. H. Cathrick, just returned in 1928 to Armoury Road from a world tour with two 986 cc sidecar outfits that had covered 45,000 miles (24,000 over land), and visited 24 countries in 19 months.*

Chapter 4

Sporting times

'Thou shalt not covet, but tradition approves all forms of competition' — *A. H. Clough*

Within six months of their launching, 3½ hp BSAs were selling well, being, as one observer remarked, easily distinguishable among rival mounts by their yellow and green-painted tanks. A reporter, visiting the Redditch works in July 1911 to watch production under way, was much impressed by the meticulous viewing and gauging methods in use to ensure reliability. 'Should an error be found,' he wrote, 'the workman who was responsible for it is fined for the fault, a rule which in itself encourages the men to put their best work into every part.'

In an end-of-season review of progress through 1911, *The Motor Cycle* commented that 'The BSA motor-bicycle has won its way to the fore during its year's existence. Next year a TT free-engine model will be made.'

For the 1912 range there were, in fact, no great changes. The rather elaborate magneto box was dispensed with, Bosch having introduced an instrument that required no waterproofing. The two-speed rear hub gear, initially announced in vague terms, had evidently been protected by adequate patents for it was offered as an alternative to the free-engine device. By means of a double cone clutch and an epicyclic gear train it provided 33 per cent reduction on the normal 'top' gear between engine pulley and belt rim. Control was either by handlebar lever and Bowden cable or by pedal and rod, the two methods being interlinked. There was also an all-chain drive model, described as being suitable for side-car work; it had long footboards and a 'foot starter'.

Pictures of the predicted TT model showed a mount differing outwardly from the standard 3½ hp machine only in that it had curved, dropped bars. There were, however, no BSAs in the 1912 TT races, nor did the marque make any noticeable impact on the sporting events of that year.

It is worth mentioning at this juncture that the Tourist Trophy races, started in 1907, had by 1912 become the premier competition in the international motor-cycling calendar, and it was customary for manufacturers to include a 'TT model' in their ranges, quite irrespective of any actual association with the Isle of Man. Often, all that was done was to strip a standard machine

of its touring equipment, fit narrow mudguards and curvaceous handlebars — and add a pound or two to the price in the hope of catching a share of the market among the sporty boys.

That the first BSA machines hardly ever appeared in competitions is not surprising, for the factory was too engrossed in building up its output to concern itself with sporting events, and the customers were mainly attracted by the touring and ride-to-work merits of the machines.

Nevertheless, rival manufacturers — notably Matchless, Triumph and Humber — were enhancing their reputations through successes in the TT and other events with machines that were still, to all intents and purposes, really only adapted versions of their ordinary standard productions, very little different, basically, from BSA's own models. A feeling that 'anything you can do, I can do better' must have arisen at Small Heath and Redditch, for an exploratory venture into the speed world was made with a singleton entry in the season-opening Easter Monday Brooklands meeting of 1913. By this time, the Weybridge track had been in existence for half a dozen years and the competition there was fierce among the established *habitués:* the chances for an untried newcomer were slim. Nonetheless, Kenneth Holden's 3½ hp BSA gained an easy win in the first race, averaging 60.75 mph, and beating a finishing field of 21 that included experts like Frank Butler (Rudge) and Harry Collier (Matchless), who were second and third. *The Motor Cycle* commented that 'Holden's win on the BSA was a great surprise, and we congratulate his firm's successful debut in racing.' Holden was the firm's head tester.

Shortly afterwards, in the Motor Cycle Club's Whitsun London-Edinburgh-London run, BSA had their first big reliability trial success when that GOM of motor-cycle sport, F. W. 'Pa' Applebee (a partner in the important BSA dealership, Godfreys of Great Portland Street) took his 3½ hp solo through the double journey without penalty to collect a gold medal.

Having made their mark both on the track and in a trial, BSA essayed the TT, with mounts that 'bristled with ingenious little fittings and additions'.

A new, raked frame was evolved; there were two-gallon petrol and half-gallon oil tanks with large diameter filler caps; a two-way tap at the base of the hand oil-pump had pipes leading to the crankcase and to a two-speed, constant-mesh gearbox mounted on the chain stays and operated by a tankside lever; transmission was all-chain with an engine-shaft shock absorber, but no clutch; a cable-controlled band brake was fitted to the front wheel and the dummy belt-rim rear brake was operated by pedals on each side of the machine. A quickly adjustable main jet in the carburettor and a novel form of tappet adjustment were the chief changes in the power department. Each tappet was in two parts, the upper member being engaged with one of four steps cut in the lower one, and held by a spring-mounted locking pin. Clearances could be set instantly by finger and thumb.

No fewer than seven BSAs were entered in the 1913 TT, which was the first, and only, two-stage race. All competitors, Seniors and Juniors, contested the first day and the survivors had a second go two days later. It was also the first year in which a Manufacturers' Team Prize was awarded. Ariel, Indian, Matchless, Norton, Premier, Quadrant, Rudge and Triumph were all competing for the new prize but, for some reason undisclosed, BSA did not enter a team — which saved them the cost of the entry fee for, in the end, only one of the septet completed the two days of racing. Their sole finisher was R. Carey, from Ireland, who came 17th, averaging 41.89 mph, as against the winning 48.28 mph of Tim Wood (Scott).

The other BSA riders were A. G. Fenn, K. Holden, R. M. Lewis, J. Steele Jnr, J. R. Thompson and F. Turvey Jnr. Archie Fenn was one of the acknowledged experts, having ridden an Ariel in the 1910 race and finished eighth on a Humber in 1911. Fred Turvey, too, had IoM experience. Kenneth Holden's mount lost its bottom gear before the start and he got no farther than Braddan on the other ratio. Steele broke a handlebar; Turvey burst a rear tyre and his flywheels came loose on the first lap of the second day, when Fenn completed two laps before retiring. An Austrian rider, G. Herman, who covered four laps, had a two-speed BSA gearbox fitted to his Puch.

The team prize, incidentally, went to the Rover company, who had entered only three machines.

In July, the French Grand Prix was held on the Picardy Circuit, near Amiens, and BSAs were ridden by Archie Fenn and Jack Woodhouse, and Frenchmen Delaune and Isodi. Fenn and Isodi finished third and sixth and Fenn had the distinction of making the fastest time through a measured one-kilometre stretch at 60.27 mph. In the same month, in the Scottish Six Days Trial, there were three BSAs in a field of 106 starters. Fenn and L. L. Sealey had two-speed jobs and Jimmy Steele's mount was a direct belt-driver. Fenn won a gold medal, as he did in the ACU's Six Days Trial held in Lakeland in August, when he lost no marks and his figure of merit, calculated on the results of various special tests, was second best to that of Rex Mundy (Triumph). On BSAs, 'Pa' Applebee and Maurice Breese gained bronze medals and H. F. Edwards, Vernon Taylor and Leonard Sealey all finished the course.

At Brooklands, in September, Kenneth Holden, riding an 85 × 88 mm 3½ hp belt-driven BSA with a sidecar and passenger, broke the track's five-mile sidecar record at 50.56 mph. The previous holder was Howard Riddell, whose 3¾ hp Zenith Gradua had averaged 49.05 mph.

With the year nearing its end, BSA announced their programme for 1914. An all single-cylinder range, it was headed by a new 4¼ hp 557 cc (85 × 98 mm) machine. With its desaxé, pear-shaped cylinder, it was similar to the 3½ hp model except in the 10 mm longer stroke, and was offered as being specially suitable for sidecar work, having a strengthened frame. An engine-shaft shock absorber, with three compression and three recoil springs, was fitted, along with a new three-speed, constant-mesh, kick-start gearbox in which were undercut sliding dogs. Within the box was also a multi-plate clutch (20 bronze and 19 steel plates) operated by a heel-and-toe pedal. Gear-shifting was done by a quadrant lever mounted on the lower tank rail, and a curious drill was required for starting off. Having freed the clutch, the rider engaged bottom gear and then kicked the engine to life, afterwards taking up the drive by the pedal. Once under way, gear changes were made by using the exhaust valve lifter. Both driving chains were encased; lubrication was through a Best and Lloyd drip-feed hand-pump and, as with all the other models except the TT type, 26 × 2½ in tyres were fitted. The price of the newcomer was £63.

Standard equipment for all the 1914 models was a Ruthardt magneto and a BSA carburettor with the petrol intake at the top of the float chamber. The other models were the 3½ hp chain-cum-belt machine with the new three-speed gearbox, a 3½ hp belt-driver with either the two-speed hub or free-engine clutch, and the direct-belt TT model, which had footrests and dropped bars, and cost £48 10s.

BSAs would be available to riders in the IOM, and that a Froude water brake was being installed to test the engines. The company made three official entries in the TT, which that year had returned to the former system of separate races for Juniors and Seniors. Innovations were the siting of the start and finish line at the top of Bray Hill and the compulsory use of ACU-approved safety helmets, which could, if so desired, be coloured according to machine makes, eg, Indian, red; Sunbeam, black and gold; Rudge, silver; Premier, yellow and blue; BSA, yellow.

Entered by the works were R. Carey, R. M. Lewis and a newcomer, F. A. Maylott. Lewis' machine had chain-belt drive, the others being all-chain. Self-entered were D. Young, G. W. Baker and S. F. Garrett, with chain-belt machines, and F. Shakespeare and Irishman J. Healey with full chain equipment. Kenneth Holden was nominated as a reserve rider, but he did not compete.

Although not in any way spectacular, the BSAs generally acquitted themselves creditably, despite experiencing more than a fair share of plug trouble. By mid-race Dan Young and Jack Healey were lying 23rd and 28th. Sidney Garrett would have been better placed had he not been delayed for several minutes at the pits struggling to undo a plug terminal. He was, perhaps, the most experienced man in the camp, having in the two previous years finished 18th and eighth on Regal-Green machines.

The Senior race was won by Cyril Pullin (Rudge) at 49.49 mph. Young got a gold medal for his 12th place at 45.47 mph and Healey, who did an extra lap, not having seen the finish flag, was placed 20th. Carey was 23rd; Frank Shakespeare, who had taken a toss at Ramsey Hairpin on the last lap, was 28th, with Garrett 34th and Maylott 44th. Only two retirements, Lewis and George Baker, out of eight starters was an encouraging improvement on the 1913 result.

The improvement was, it transpired, even greater than it had appeared to be for, after the *provisional* results had been published, the ACU disqualified the men who had occupied 18th and 40th positions, so all the other riders who finished behind them moved up accordingly; this made Healey 19th, Carey 22nd, Shakespeare 27th, Garrett 33rd and Maylott 42nd.

The Irish End-to-End trial, run over 506 miles in July, saw the BSA riders W. J. Woods, C. Jones and W. J. Chambers win the team prize.

However, there were war-like noises in the air, and the International Six Days Trial, centred on Grenoble, in which Maurice Breese was the only BSA entrant, was cancelled. The same thing happened to the French Grand Prix, in which Brown Brothers Ltd had entered a BSA team.

The last major sporting event for English motor cyclists before Great Britain and France declared war on Germany was the MCC's hill-climbing and holiday run, from August 1 to 3 in the Peak District; the winner of the Solo Cup was G. P. Howe (557 BSA).

In November, when it should have been full of motor cycles, Olympia was being used for the incarceration of German aliens.

Chapter 5

Wartime expansion

'Progress . . . is not an accident, but a necessity' — *Herbert Spencer.*

August 1914 saw the Birmingham Small Arms Company back at full tilt on its original business of gun-making. The demand was fantastic, for the War Office had allowed weapon stocks to dwindle alarmingly; indeed, it was actually caught in the process of discarding the old Mark III Short Lee-Enfield rifle, first introduced in 1907, in favour of a type based, believe it or not, on the German Mauser.

With 24-hour shifts working seven days a week, Small Heath and the associated factories increased production from 650 to 4,360 rifles a week and in two years this had risen to 8,000, with a peak by the war's end of 10,000. Throughout World War I BSA produced over a million and a half Short Lee-Enfields and enough spares to make another half million. In a new factory at Small Heath, always afterwards called the New Building, the company was also manufacturing Lewis machine guns at a rate that reached 2,000 a week. The only makers of the Lewis gun, BSA supplied the British, Russian and Belgian forces and the total war production was 145,397 complete weapons, together with huge quantities of spare parts.

At the same time military bicycles were pouring from the plant. The Army Cyclist Corps made great use of bicycles and was soon demanding an ultra-lightweight machine that could be easily carried over terrain too rough for riding. BSA technicians designed a folding cycle that could be carried on a soldier's back, leaving his hands free for rifle and grenade use.

The motor-cycle workshops, too, were at full stretch. The strength and slogging power of Beesa* machines were proved over and over again, not only on the war-torn roads of Flanders and France, but also in German East Africa where 400 machines supplied to the South African Motor Cycle Corps were flogged through rivers, sand, swamps and mud under conditions no trials organiser would ever have dreamed up.

Yet, in spite of all the military urgency, BSA

*Commonly accepted alternatives are Beeza and Besa, the latter being the official name of 7.9 mm and 15 mm machine guns, 60,500 of which were made by BSA during World War II.

continued, as did many other motor-cycle makers, to supply the civilian market. The 1915 range was described in November 1914, three months after the start of hostilities, as containing no radical changes. The 3½ hp engine was now fitted only to the TT model but it, and the 4¼ hp type, had a caged roller big-end bearing. Details were also given of a new 2½ hp side-valve model, having dimensions of 68 × 68 mm, 247 cc, with the valves enclosed in separate cases. The magneto was mounted behind the cylinder and transmission was by chain and belt through a three-speed gearbox having ratios of 5.7, 8.5 and 15.9 to 1. There was no clutch or kickstarter. The machine was, said the company, still being tested and there was no intention of marketing it before the spring, when the probable price would be £42.

Except to give news of personalities who were on war service, the motor-cycle press had little to say about BSA until October 1915, when it was stated that the 1916 range would be 'much as before', though painted in an all-black austerity livery. The TT model was still listed, now with a variable engine-pulley. The 557 cc types were called the Model H if fitted with all-chain drive, or the Model K if chain-cum-belt; prices were respectively £64 and £62. There was no mention of the promised 250 cc side-valve machine.

A Ministry of Munitions Order, issued in November 1916, prohibited 'the manufacture or repair, without a permit, of any machine designed for mechanical transport or traction'. Since permits were obtainable only for essential war work, all business in civilian machines was suspended for two years until the 1918 Armistice.

By this time BSA's workforce at the Small Heath, Redditch and Sparkbrook factories had increased from 3,500 to over 13,000 employees. The factory capacity had been doubled and trebled and the company, having become one of the world's largest light engineering concerns, had to be reorganised completely for peace-time production. This was done by separating the cycle, gun and tool-making activities into individual sections and at the end of January 1919 it was given out that 'In future the manufacture of BSA motor cycles and bicycles will be run by a company separate from the Birmingham Small Arms Co Ltd, which will be known as BSA Cycles Ltd. Mr C. A. Hyde, the manager of the cycle and motor-cycle department of the parent concern, will be managing director. Mr Hyde, one of the best-known figures in the trade, invented the Hyde free-wheel. Now that Government contracts are about to terminate, the whole of the enormous surplus factory space and plant will be adapted to the construction of cycles and motor cycles on a scale hitherto unprecedented.'

Ten months later BSA introduced their first V-twin, the Model E — a 6-7 hp side-valver that was the forerunner of a series of powerful multi-cylinder mounts which were to earn world-wide respect for faithful, dependable service. That the newcomer was claimed to be the result of three years' experiment suggested that it had originally been intended for the 1916 market and that production had been halted by the ban on civilian construction.

Certainly, there was nothing revolutionary about its design. The 76 × 85 mm, 770 cc, engine had the cylinders set at a 50-degree angle and, as with the single-cylinder models, the valves were interchangeable, having quickly adjustable tappets. The constant-loss lubrication system employed a mechanical pump, with an emergency hand pump. An Amac carburettor was used and ignition was by a chain-driven EIC magneto or Lucas Magdyno. The long-skirted pistons each carried two compression and two scraper rings; H-section con-rods had phosphor-bronze small-ends and rollers in the big-ends.

Transmission was by chains enclosed in cast-aluminium cases, with BSA's own design of shock-absorber on the engine shaft. A seven-plate Ferodo-faced clutch was provided for the redesigned constant-mesh three-speed gearbox that incorporated a kickstarter. Detachable and interchangeable wheels were fitted with 26 × 3 in tyres, shrouded by big mudguards. The saddle was mounted on a spring-loaded column telescoping within the seat pillar. An immensely strong frame had a new type of cantilever front fork in which a single compression spring superseded the original 'push-pull' device. The solo weight of the machine was 336 lb.

Although deliveries were not promised until the following spring, the twin was exhibited at the 1919 Olympia Show, with a price ticket of £130. The 557 cc single-cylinder type was shown with all-chain drive at £110 or, in chain-belt form, at £107. Still available was the 499 cc single-gear

belt-drive TT model.

It is not without interest to compare the price of the 770 BSA with those of some other 6 hp V-twin rivals, viz, Bat (Jap engine), £139; Bradbury, £141; AJS, £148; Royal Enfield, £160. And a good idea of how the motor cycle market had come out of the Great War is provided by the following breakdown of types available to British buyers:

	1915	1920
Two-stroke singles	33	43
Two-stroke twins	1	1
Four-stroke singles	20	25
Four-stroke V-twins	26	28
Four-stroke flat-twins	4	8
Four-stroke fours	1	3
	85	**108**

The march of progress showed a move towards bigger tyres, increased use of rear-wheel springing and a universal adoption of all-chain drive for sidecar hauliers.

*　　*　　*

Five BSAs had competed in the 1919 Scottish Six Days Trial, gaining only one gold medal, but the marque really came to the forefront in the following September's ACU Six Days event, held around Llandrindod Wells. Using their new title for the first time in a competition, BSA Cycles Ltd entered their pre-war stalwarts F. Turvey, W. J. Chambers, H. F. Edwards. L. L. Sealey, 'Pa' Applebee and a new boy, A. E. Wood, one of Charles Hyde's Redditch staff who devoted his working life to BSA and later played an important part in guiding its fortunes. All except Irishman Chambers, who had a 500 cc sidecar outfit, were on 557 cc mounts, contesting the 750 cc solo class. Private owners W. Edwards and H. R. Lane had 557 cc sidecar machines.

The result was a great success for the Piled Arms. H. F. Edwards, Sealey and Turvey, with a merit score totalling, appropriately, 557 points, won the team prize, a Scott-riding trio being second with 539 points. 'Pa' Applebee, then in his 60th year, Edwards and Turvey all gained gold medals. Silver tokens went to Sealey and Chambers, and Wood and W. Edwards retired only after they had reached the mid-week stage.

Maintaining their form, Sealey, Edwards and Turvey all collected 'golds' in the 1920 'Scottish' and the other three BSA men, Chambers, W. Buchan and W. Edwards, each losing only one mark, were silver-medal winners. In the autumn ACU Six Days Trial all five of the BSA riders finished with clean sheets, the best performance in the trial being made by Fred Turvey.

Ninety-five individual manufacturers exhibited at the 1920 Show, when the BSA range showed little change. The 500 cc model had disappeared. The 557 cc machines now had revised, quieter timing gear, and front forks and gearboxes as per the twin, which was given bigger mudguards and a price rise to £150. Specially designed to pair with it was a sidecar having a triangulated chassis with a transverse, half-elliptic leaf-spring to carry the body. Price of the complete outfit was £189.

Commenting on 'What I rode in 1920', the celebrated sage of *The Motor Cycle,* 'Ixion', said of the 557 cc BSA: 'I did not know that a single-cylinder could develop so much power. I never unearthed a gradient that could bring her down to first, using that gear only for starting off. And talk about substantial! The BSA is built like a tank, and is fundamentally incapable of fracturing anything, whilst she creates the pleasant impression that nothing will ever wear out.'

All five of the BSA works riders in the 1921 Scottish Six Days were gold medalists, among them being B. L. 'Bertie' Bird, a redoubtable sidecar driver whose earlier reputation as a Quadrant exponent was further enhanced when he transferred his allegiance to Small Heath. In the silver-medal list appeared the name of W. L. Handley (OK Junior). It was the first time Walter Handley, then employed by Humphries and Dawes as a delivery-messenger boy, made his mark in a major motor-cycle competition. Sixteen years later, when he had reached the height of his road-racing fame, he had one ride on a BSA that made an astonishing impact on the course of the company's development — as we shall see in due course.

In May 1921, Charles Hyde resigned his post as managing director of BSA Cycles Ltd, through ill health, and he was succeeded by Commander Godfrey Herbert, DSO.

Chapter 6

The terrible TT

'. . . he who never made a mistake, never made a discovery' — *Samuel Smiles*

There had been no BSAs in the 1920 TT; it was intended that there should be, but the project had gone awry. Under what was, hopefully, a mantle of secrecy, the experimental department had been testing at Brooklands an entirely new design that was expected to run away with the first post-war Island event. Of course, nothing that happened at the Track could really be kept secret for long, and it was soon revealed that the racer had a 500 cc, four-valve, alloy-head, sloping engine mounted in a duplex-tube frame. Had this machine been raced in 1920 it would have predated the renowned four-valve Ricardo Triumph. However, its performance was not up to expectations and the TT entry was withheld to give time for concentration on a fresh layout.

Early in June 1921 the 'Blue 'Un' (*The Motor Cycle*) prefaced a long and rather prolix description of the revised version by saying: 'For something like 12 months the BSA company has succeeded in maintaining the secret of its Tourist Trophy motor cycles. Originally intended for the 1920 event, the machines have been undergoing a long course of trial and, consequently, although the design is distinctly unorthodox in appearance, all the features have been thoroughly tried out'.

More forthrightly, the 'Green 'Un' (*Motor Cycling*) said it had known about the plot all along but had refrained from mentioning it, 'being under a bond of secrecy' — despite the fact that it had published details of the four-valver when it first arrived at Brooklands. Both journals, however, were agreed that BSA had produced a light, economical and very easily controllable machine, 'capable,' it was said, 'of speeds which should be sufficient to win the Island race . . . and the chances of the BSA are much too good to be neglected'. That it was found, when weighed on the ACU's scales, to be, at 310 lb, the heaviest machine in its class, was by the way.

Nevertheless, this 499 cc (85 × 88 mm) single was a most advanced and praiseworthy attempt to break away from the current fashion. During the 12-month experimental session the overhead gear had been completely redesigned to a plan that incorporated two vertical valves working in a detachable, unfinned iron cylinder head, and the method of their operation was, indeed, highly unorthodox. Each rocker was set east-west-wise across the head and was supported on its under side by the valve stem and tubular pushrod (which had a coil return spring at its foot). A knife-edge, formed on the upper side of the rocker, engaged in a V-groove cut in an overhanging, square-section bar that was mounted in T-form on a single support post screwed into the head. There was no kind of lubrication whatever. Both valves had hollow stems and the inlet was of semi-tulip shape. Large diameter, square-section springs were retained by caps secured by split conical thimbles which, being screwed on to the valve stems, also provided clearance adjustment. Except for special cams, the timing gear used standard components.

On a fully floating gudgeon pin an aluminium slipper piston, considerably cut away at the sides, carried only one ring, its scraper effect being aided by a series of holes drilled in the groove. Steel flywheels and an oscillating-plunger oil pump were the only changes from standard practice in the 'bottom half'. There was a crankcase-pressure relief-valve supply to the primary chain. 'It is expected,' prophesied *The Motor Cycle*, 'that this system will be sufficient for the needs of the race, but in case of emergencies a foot-operated oil pump is connected directly to the crankcase'.

The breathing arrangements were also unusual. To the exhaust port was attached a Y-shaped alloy manifold that allowed long tail pipes to clear the front down tubes on each side of the machine. The BSA carburettor, with handlebar-controlled adjustable main jet and horizontal double barrels, was mounted remotely, just above the gearbox at the end of a lengthy, dog-legged intake.

The engine was mounted very low and far forward at a slightly inclined angle in a duplex-tube frame, the top tubes and saddle stays forming a straight line from steering head to rear hub. The resulting, remarkably low, seat position was claimed not only to aid navigation but also to be 'comfortable'. The semi-wedge shaped tank held two gallons of petrol, and a gallon of oil was carried in a container behind the seat pillar.

The rest of the specification was more or less standard. Starter-less, the gearbox had close ratios (4.1, 5.6 and 8.2:1); the front fork was of usual BSA type; braking was on dummy belt rims on both wheels, the rear being operated by pedals on each side of the machine. Originally, 650 × 65 mm tyres were used; there were light guards over the chains; a carrier with two tool-boxes; rear stand; and, 'as an instance of the thoroughness of the design', there were nail-catchers fore and aft.

To ride the new racers, BSA Cycles Ltd chose and entered a squad of eight men, most of whom already had TT experience, or were factory employees. T. E. Greene, from Ireland, had ridden Rudges in 1913 and '14; G. Kuhn had finished second on a Levis in the 250 cc class of the 1920 Lightweight Race; F. C. North was an Ariel veteran from pre-war races; H. Riddell had raced a Calthorpe in the 1914 Senior; T. Simister had been in the Norton camp in 1920; A. E. Taylor had never been to the Island but, as a young BSA apprentice, had shown signs of riding skill. Both from the Redditch factory, A. E. Wood (who had succeeded Holden as head tester) and H. Poole (chief draughtsman) were nominated as reserve riders.

Under the team managership of Commander St John, these men established themselves in Ramsey's Queen's Hotel, and duly turned out for practising. At that time, to relieve pressure on accommodation in Douglas, the ACU encouraged competitors to make their headquarters in the Island's northern town, those that did so being allowed to start their early morning laps by joining the course at Parliament Square.

On the third morning Tommy Greene had got on the leaderboard, with a lap in 45 min 58 sec, behind a quintet composed of Nortons, Indians and a Sunbeam. Observers' initial impressions were that the BSAs had exceptionally good acceleration and a fair turn of speed but, as the training proceeded, the riders complained of steering difficulties, and bigger front wheels with 26 × 3 in tyres were fitted to improve the rake effect.

Then, mid-way through practising, Albert Wood and Gus Kuhn crashed together near Waterworks Corner. They had been trying out the comparative performances of BSA and Amac carburettors. Wood quickly recovered from mild injuries, but Kuhn had so damaged an ankle that he was confined to his hotel room. He had the bed moved to the window, from which he could shower caustic comments on the tuning efforts of his colleagues in the yard below.

There is another story, which sounds as though it might be true, about that yard. Ordinarily it was used as a parking place for a large, locally owned Minerva limousine. To give themselves more elbow-room, the TT boys used to push the car across the promenade on to a boatmen's slipway. One hot afternoon, having finished their work on the bikes, they went to retrieve the Minerva — only to find that it had slipped — on sun-melted tar — down the ramp and was half submerged by the incoming tide!

The BSA crew had plenty of work to do for, having improved the steering of their machines, they had come up against repeated problems with the engines. First, Harold Poole had his cylinder crack, and thereafter, right up to weighing-in time, it was a perpetual struggle to keep six mounts in service. 'Apparently,' according to *Motor Cycling,* 'the engines give off such phenomenal power that the parts are not strong enough to stand it. Pistons, valves and cylinders have all had to be changed'.

On race day, Gus Kuhn was not fit enough to ride and Albert Wood took his place on the grid. Bert Taylor, first of the BSA squad to face the starter, had a long, hard push before his engine fired. The noise of Charlie North's exhaust was noted as 'a thing to be wondered at'.

Misfiring all the way, Taylor succeeded in covering two laps and when he seized up on Bray Hill the other five were already retired — all of them with 'engine trouble'. Howard Riddell raised a laugh when he rode in past the Grandstand on a push-bike. Up on the Mountain there were also fun and games, reported by one of *Motor Cycling's* men stationed at Keppel Gate. 'Two amusing incidents occurred at this point,' he wrote. 'A BSA spanner flew out of a machine as it whirled by at speed, and hit a spectator, who thereupon fell backwards from a precarious perch. Then one of the marshals became involved in a catch-as-catch-can chase with a spectator who wanted to cross the road'.

But for BSA there was nothing to laugh at at all, and even at this far distance in time one trembles to think of the icy reception that must have greeted the lads when they returned to Small Heath. Two years of expensive development work had brought nothing but ignominy, and a decade of patient endeavour to build a reputation for reliability had been jeopardised in one disastrous morning.

'Never again,' said the directors, and they

stuck to their ruling for, henceforth, nothing could persuade the company to re-enter the lists of international road racing.

* * *

Through the sitting-room window of his comfortable Worcestershire home at Chaddesley Corbett, Bert Taylor contemplated the distant view of the Malvern Hills as he sent his mind back over 55 years to that Island debacle.

'So far as I was concerned,' he told me, 'it all began in 1920 when I was working as a road tester at the Redditch factory where the experimental department had been preparing some machines for that year's TT. I don't think I ever saw one completed but, because I had shown some ability as a rider, I was offered £500 to compete in the race — and I wasn't even 20! But the team was withdrawn and, whatever they said otherwise, the reason for that was because the bikes couldn't be got ready in time on account of a strike in the moulding shop! I claimed my £500 and, after a lot of argument, I got it, together with the threat of the sack if I bothered them any more. Meanwhile, new machines were being made and when the 1921 race came up I was told I had to ride; no more argument — and no more money.

'Harry Poole, whose boss was Dick Nicholls, the works manager, produced the frames and cycle parts at Redditch and the engines were built at the Sparkbrook works to the designs of two men who had had Great War experience with aero engines — their names were Pearsall and Heather. Donald Heather, of course, went on to become one of the chiefs at Associated Motor Cycles in Woolwich.

'Although the race machines were said to have been thoroughly tried out, they hadn't really had any road testing. BSA had a shed at Brooklands, and on the track, ridden by Howard Riddell, those early 'slopers' appeared to perform well. But there's a lot of difference between occasional short bursts of speed on the concrete and a hammering over the Mountain Course — as we soon found out when we got to the Island. The steering was dreadful — they wagged their tails alarmingly, and because of the low tank we had nothing to get a grip on with our legs. We got over that by putting a block of wood on the tank top and strapping knee-grips round it.

'But, by golly, they could go — unfortunately not for long! The acceleration was terrific and they would reach 70 in second gear, but I never dared find out what was maximum in top. Steering was improved a bit by fitting different-sized wheels and tyres, but the engines gave constant trouble. Throughout practising none of us ever did more than two consecutive laps before something went wrong. Seizing up was the main problem, and you could almost predict where it would happen. We had started with cast-iron pistons, and then Victor Horsman, who was closely in touch with Harry Ricardo, sportingly provided us with special alloy slipper jobs with concave crowns.

'But that didn't cure all the troubles. Valves broke, and, if they didn't seize, the engines got so hot that the aluminium Y-shaped exhaust manifolds melted; we looped the pushrods together with bits of string, so that when one rod flew out we didn't lose it. Rocker-to-valve clearance was set by a conical thimble screwed on to the stem and mating with the valve-spring cap. To try to stop them unscrewing, we painted them with sal-ammoniac, hoping they would rust up solid!'

Bert broke off his recollections, rummaged in a drawer and produced a knife-edge rocker and a spring cap, both pretty rusty.

'We took 14 racers to Ramsey,' he continued, 'and brought back 14 wrecks. One was kept at Redditch; the others were rebuilt and disposed of. I should think that these two bits are about all that's left of what was really a very fast layout. If only it had been put through a proper development programme, it could have been a winner. But it's better to learn to run before you race — especially in the Isle of Man!'

Bert Taylor, whose son now manages his several West Midlands motor businesses, is well qualified to pass that judgment. He rode in seven more TTs and crowned his career with a second place in the 1925 Sidecar race. And, at 75, he is still a regular spectator.

Chapter 7

Round Tank, Super Sports and Sloper

'New things are made familiar, and familiar things are made new' — *Dr Johnson*

Not surprisingly, when BSA announced their 1922 range there was no mention of any TT model. Instead, 'speed merchants' were offered a specially tuned Sports version of the 557 cc Model H, listed, like its touring companion, at £110. The chain-belt Model K cost £107 and the 6 hp 770 cc Model E, £132. Major changes in specification were a new design of front fork which had a central, barrel compression spring, very much like the Webb pattern but with curved main girders, and a forged-steel steering head to replace the malleable cast-iron lug. Thus, the only castings in BSA motor cycles were now the iron cylinders and the aluminium crankcases, gearbox shells and chain enclosures.

New for 1922 was an 8 hp V-twin, progenitor of a long-lasting type that, in harness with heavyweight sidecars, gave faithful service through the 1920s and 1930s. A 986 cc (80 × 98 mm) side-valve engine was fitted in a frame similar to that of the 770 cc model, but having the single-spring cantilever front fork. Dummy belt-rim brakes were still used but there was also a drum brake in the rear chain wheel. Long footboards, sit-up-and-beg bars, huge mudguards and a leaf-spring saddle were standard features; complete with sidecar (it was not sold as a solo), the Model F cost £185 and the unladen weight, including a spare wheel, was close on 600 lb. Cruising at about 45-50 mph, the 'Beesa combo', as it was affectionately known, gave many happy families the opportunity to explore, cheaply and independently, their own countryside.

Since the Armistice the company had been expanding into a group organisation. The Daimler division had acquired a big, six-storey building on the Coventry road, near Hay Mills, to make a new range of BSA-Daimler light cars. These had 1,100 cc, air-cooled, ohv V-twin Hotchkiss engines and were good runners. The Group also bought up several well-established companies whose products were allied to, or could aid, BSA interests, and one was Sheffield's oldest steel firm, Wm Jessop and Sons.

However, all the bright hopes were dimmed when the post-war depression began to have its effect, and BSA shareholders found themselves without a dividend. Indeed, in the 21-year period between the two World Wars the company paid dividends on only eight occasions, and more than once employees had to accept salary cuts. The picture seemed to brighten a little when, in April 1923, it was announced that 'the balance sheet just published shows a deficit of only £42,206, as against £336,000 the previous year'. Directors of the parent company were then A. Neville Chamberlain, MP, Sir Hallewell Rogers, W. L. Baylay, A. Eadie, P. Martin (USA) and T. S. Walker.

Nevertheless, 1922 had seen a big increase in motor-cycle production and in this year several names that were to become familiar in the BSA story appeared for the first time in the public prints.

In the Colmore Cup trial the rider of a 4¼ hp solo, H. S. Perrey, was reported to have won a silver medal. It was because of a small advertisement in a Birmingham paper that Harry Perrey had become involved with Small Heath and, 56 years later, over the tea-cups in his Moseley home, he told me how it happened. Returned from Army service in India, he, like thousands of others, was getting desperate for a civilian job when, in 1920, he spotted a couple of lines in the Sits Vac column — 'Ex-officer, keen motor cyclist, wanted by leading company. Particulars, Box No . . .'

Harry got the job which, it turned out, was to act as assistant to F. W. Hulse, Small Heath's brilliant engineer who was not only in charge of all design work but also played an important part on the production side. Freddie Hulse was not satisfied with the way things were going at the Redditch plant and Harry Perrey's task was to 'seek out and report back'. He didn't relish it much, and when he got the chance to show his ability as a trialsman he grabbed it, and was soon the company's leading rider, organising and managing BSA's first competitions department, a section entirely separate from the experimental shop. One of his incidental duties was to road-test all the rebuilt 1921 TT machines before they were dispatched to their new owners. In the 1922 Scottish Six Days Trial Perrey was one of five BSA riders who gained gold medals and was a member of the prize-winning manufacturers' team.

BSA ran a trial for their own staff in May — starting from Armoury Road, including many of the well-known Cotswold hills and finishing at Stratford-upon-Avon. Among the 75 competitors were J. Leek and F. Howard, both on 6 hp side-car outfits and both reported to have made particularly good climbs of Saintbury Hill. James Leek, who was destined to lead BSA to tremendous heights of achievement in World War II, was then the firm's planning officer; Howard was chief of the accounts office. Len Sealey made best solo performance and A. C. Kerkhoff, the press-shop foreman, won the sidecar prize.

Two girl trials riders, the Debenham sisters, Nancy and Betty, began a lengthy association with BSA at this time.

New Sports models, developed and built at Redditch, appeared in the range for 1923 — 350 and 500 cc side-valvers. The 350, priced at £57 15s, had dimensions of 72 × 85.5 mm, 349 cc. Its cams operated directly on the tappet feet; lubrication was by a mechanical pump driven off the inlet camshaft and delivering oil through a tank-top sight-feed to the forward side of the cylinder. The gearbox was a scaled-down version of the three-speed countershaft component that had been in use since 1920. At first there was a metal-to-metal internal-expanding brake on the front wheel, but this was changed before the Olympia Show to a dummy belt-rim type, similar to that on the rear wheel. A maximum speed of 50 mph at 3,800 rpm was claimed. At £70, with bore and stroke of 80 × 98 mm (493 cc), the larger machine differed otherwise only in having the full-size gearbox and lever cam followers.

The 4¼, 6 and 8 hp range was as before except that 'simplified' (less equipment and cheaper) editions of the twins were available as the Light Six and Light Eight.

Around this period the motor-cycle industry had got itself into a ferocious price-cutting war and, concurrently with the release of details of the 1924 programme, BSA proclaimed 'a bold step towards stabilising trading conditions'. They guaranteed that the prices announced at the Show would be maintained throughout the whole of the season and that there would be no alterations in design.

The next bold, though hardly stabilising, step was made in January 1924 when BSA knocked the market sideways with a motor cycle that cost less than £40 — the ever-famous, 'Round Tank' Lightweight Model B.

Motor Cycling greeted this bonny baby as fol-lows: 'The latest addition to the already comprehensive range of BSA machines is an extremely sturdy and attractive lightweight that costs but £39 10s, scales some 170 lb and is capable of a speed of about 45 mph'.

Below the cylindrical tank, metal-strapped to the top rail, was a side-valve 63 × 80 mm, 249 cc unit of simple design, with ball and plain main bearings, a roller-bearing big-end and a flat-top aluminium piston. The magneto platform-cum-gear-drive casing was cast in one with the right-side crankcase half and the idler wheel in the gear train drove a mechanical oil pump situated in the cover plate. An enclosed-chain primary drive included a cam-faced shock-absorber and a floating dry-plate clutch on a two-speed gearbox. Standard ratios were 6.25 and 11.61:1, but an alternative sprocket could be supplied to give lower gears for riders living in hilly country.

There were also two styles of handlebar — sports and touring — with no inverted control levers. Gears were changed by a long lever attached directly to the box. Braking was on the rear wheel only, two independently operated blocks acting on the dummy belt rim. BSA had to go to court to prove that the system was, indeed, independent, as the law required. Unusually small, 24 in diameter, wheels had 2¼ in-section tyres, well mudguarded, and the equipment included adjustable footrests, a carrier, a big toolbox and stands front and back. An astonishing average of 120 mpg, on a 4.8:1 compression ratio, was attainable.

'It is expected,' said *Motor Cycling* enthusiastically, 'that the thoroughly practical nature of this so low-priced, yet roadworthy, little machine will secure for it many friends. We venture to predict a rosy future for it'.

How right they were! Using mass-production methods for the first time, BSA built and sold 15,000 machines in the next 12 months and when the run ended some four years later, by which time three speeds and a rectangular tank were available, 35,000 Lightweights had spread all over the world.

Barely a fortnight after the shock debut of the Model B, BSA launched another surprise — the company's first overhead-valve roadster, which was also the first complete motor cycle to be constructed wholly at Small Heath. It was a 350 cc vertical single, and Harry Perrey remembers its inception. Freddie Hulse, it seems, had taken a close look at the Hotchkiss engine which powered the BSA light car, and was so impressed with its cylinder and head layout that he decided it could well be adapted to motor-cycle use. Harold Briggs, a clever technician who had come to Small Heath from the Daimler works at Coventry, undertook the job, reproducing the relevant Hotchkiss features to suit bore and stroke measurements of 72 × 85.5 mm, 349 cc.

A detachable, hemispherical, iron cylinder head had heavy finning, carried well forward around an extended exhaust port. Long-stemmed, tulip valves, inclined at a narrow angle, were operated by rockers mounted in bolt-on boxes, with lids to give access for adjustment. Plated tubes enclosed the pushrods, which were made of Duralumin, the idea being that the different expansion coefficients of the iron cylinder and the Dural rods would compensate, to preserve valve clearances. A dome-topped alloy piston had three rings, and roller bearings were used in the big-end and on the timing side of the crankshaft. The rest of the specification was almost the same as that of the Sports side-valve model. Performance-wise, the ohv developed 13 bhp, had a top speed of 60 mph and a 100 mpg consumption figure; it weighed 220 lb and cost £59 10s.

Before the year was out there was a 493 cc big brother, equipped either as a Sports or Colonial type.

The motor-cycle section of BSA was by now well on its way to establishing its claim to be 'Leaders of the Industry', and at the end of the 1924 season a 12 months' output of 26,042 machines fully justified their advertising slogan, 'One in four is a BSA'. The size of the display at Olympia caused one of the technical journals to call it 'the most complete range ever offered by one firm'. There were a dozen basic models, all of which could be ordered with alternative specifications, and all carrying much-reduced price tickets. For the record, this was the BSA programme for 1925:

Model	cc	Type	£	s
B	249	Lightweight single	36	15
L	349	Side-valve single	43	3
L	349	Ohv Sports single	52	10
S	493	Ohv Sports single	52	10
S	493	Ohv Colonial single	52	10
H	557	Light single	62	0
H	557	De luxe single	70	0
E	770	Light twin	72	0
E	770	De luxe twin	80	0
G	986	Light twin	72	0
G	986	De luxe twin	80	0
G	986	Colonial twin	75	0

There were seven styles of sidecars, ranging from £15 to £28 for a two-seater with a sprung wheel. Improved oil pumps were fitted to the H, E and G models and the B and L types had friction-damped lower fork links. The sole remaining belt-driver, the Model K, had passed away, as had the 350 and 500 cc Sports side-valve types. Half-way through 1925, however, a very low-priced — £44 15s — 500 cc edition of the 350 cc standard side-valve machine was added to the S group.

Having stated that they would not be exhibiting at the Olympia Show, BSA published their 1926 intentions in August 1925. There were two additions to the existing fleet, a three-speed Lightweight at £37 10s, which had a black, instead of green, tank, and a Super Sports 350. Back in March, a prototype of this machine had performed well when ridden by Bertie Bird in the London-Gloucester and Colmore Cup trials.

In production form it was seen to differ from the ohv Sports mount chiefly in the valve gear. The naked steel pushrods were barrel-shaped, tapering to the ends from maximum diameter in the middle and, for extra lightness, they were bored hollow. Making them was a nice little job for BSA's gun-barrelling machinists. There were individually adjustable return springs at the lower ends of the rods and the tops engaged with rockers carried, via cup-and-cone ball bearings (bicycle-hub style), on shafts passing through the enclosing boxes. Hollow-stemmed valves had double springs and the domed aluminium piston produced a compression ratio so high — 6.8:1 — that a 50/50 mixture of petrol and aviation spirit was obligatory. An Amac carburettor was fitted. The crank assembly, which had forged-steel flywheels, ran on ball bearings on both sides, and all engines were bench-tested to peak at 5,600 rpm, which gave speeds of 70 to 73 mph. An André friction-type steering damper was used for the first time on a BSA.

The Super Sports was a very good motor cycle, remarkably successful in competitions, and it particularly proved itself in one of the many special tests of reliability and stamina to which the company submitted its machines in the 1920s (see Chapter 8).

Meantime, the Hulse-Briggs partnership had yet another winner in the stable, and in August 1926 one of the most famous motor cycles ever made began a production life that was to last almost ten years — the immortal 'Sloper', of which there are still many in good running order, lovingly maintained in near-mint condition.

Only in that it had a 500 cc, inclined, ohv engine did the new model S bear any resemblance to the earlier 'sloper', the ill-starred 1921 TT racer. In fact, it had no racing background whatsoever, and was never intended for high-speed work. But the way in which the robust power unit was blended into the low-saddle (25 in) frame produced a smart, purposeful appearance that immediately appealed to riders who were looking for a mount that filled a gap between the staid touring type and the out-and-out sportster. The Sloper had style, an excellent, quiet performance, BSA reliability, a fully up-to-date specification and cost, in Standard form, only £47 10s. There was an even classier Super Sports version, capable of 70-75 mph, at £53.

The Sloper story is so well known that there is no need to dilate on its make-up and development. In brief, the 1926-27 model had a single-port 493 cc (80 × 98 mm) cylinder mounted on a capacious crank case-sump with the magneto (or Magdyno) situated behind the barrel. Inwardly inclined, enclosed pushrods operated rockers in a box-shaped casting that left the valve springs exposed. A brazed-up, duplex-tube cradle frame was used, with a curved main-blade, friction-damped, front fork. The wedge-pattern tank carried the quadrant for the control lever to the three-speed gearbox and a specially notable feature was the braking system; the pedal actuated both 7 in diameter drums, but the handlebar lever applied the front brake only.

In the course of time a handsome, plated saddle tank arrived; a two-port exhaust system was introduced; the front fork was changed to a straight-tube type; and the top tubes gave place to a backbone-cum-steering-head steel forging. Other refinements and additions kept pace with the fashions but, in the main, the basic concept was never altered and the Sloper is today revered as a classic milestone on the road of motor-cycle progress.

Chapter 8

Proving the product

'Great things are done when men and mountains meet' — *William Blake*

About the same time that Commander Herbert became managing director of BSA Cycles Ltd, there stepped into prominence at Small Heath a man who proved over many years to be highly competent to carry out the work he had set himself to do, which was to build up and sustain at high pressure the company's 'public image', an expression unknown in those early days before the arts and crafts of propaganda had spawned such activities as press and public relations. J. W. Bryan was the advertising chief of BSA Cycles: but, whereas his opposite numbers in rival factories mostly concerned themselves with the printed media — buying space, advertisement design, catalogue and brochure production, for example — Joe Bryan developed his domain at the office end of Armoury Road into a unit capable of instigating and undertaking the kind of publicity campaigns that, in later years, became the province of specialist consultants and agencies. In short, J.W.B. was one of, if not the, first PROs in the motor-cycle business, though he would not then have understood what the letters signified.

A man of strong personality, he became known throughout the trade as 'Bully' Bryan, not out of disrespect but in recognition of his determination to press forward the progress, fortunes and good name of the Piled Arms marque. In his book, BSA meant Best, Supreme, All-powerful; and he strove mightily to uphold that creed.

The opportunities for, and the ways and means of attempting publicly to demonstrate that one make of motor cycle is better than any other are, and always have been, somewhat limited. Racing, either on road or track, may win a reputation for high-speed endurance, but it is much dependent on special skills and a large element of luck; economy, comfort and price count for little in the end product. Organised rough-country tests such as reliability trials come nearer to the object of persuading the customers that a mount so proven can be expected to give good service in a private owner's hands, but again, even in so-called stock-machine events, riding expertise plays a big part in success achievement.

For BSA racing was, at that time, taboo; on the trials scene the marque was always in the forefront. But what Bryan and his colleagues particularly wanted were unique, individual demonstrations — perhaps 'stunts' would be a more descriptive word — that could be publicised as easily comprehendable proofs of the all-round excellence of BSA motor cycles.

It wasn't a new idea. From the very earliest days of the industry, manufacturers had submitted their machines to endurance tests like End-to-End (Land's End to John o' Groats) record attacks, Round Britain rides and similar marathons. In 1923 an Exeter dealer, George Pettyt, proprietor of Maudes Motor Mart, had presented an award, at first called the Pettyt Cup and later the Maudes Trophy, to encourage the trade to undertake worthwhile demonstrations of their standard products, under strict, impartial Auto Cycle Union observation. Norton Motors were the first firm to capture the prize and they were the winners over four successive years.

Maybe the significance of the Pettyt award had escaped the notice of Small Heath for, when J.W.B. and the competitions department planned their first full-scale demo in 1924, they did not register it with the ACU as an officially observed entry for the Maudes contest, although they engaged the services of Major R. V. C. Brook, a consulting engineer who was also an approved timekeeper and one of the Union's Midland Centre officials.

The object of the exercise, held on April 4, was to show the ability of BSA motor cycles to climb what was regarded as one of the most difficult hills in the United Kingdom, Screw Hill in West Wales. A fleet of seven different models, representing the entire range, was to be employed — 250 and 350 cc side-valvers, a 350 ohv and 500, 557, 770 and 1,000 cc sidecar outfits. Some of the machines had lower-than-standard gears, but only sprockets that were available to the public were used.

Screw Hill rises from sea-level to a spur on the twin mountains, known as the Rivals, on the Caernarvonshire coast, near Nevin (Nefyn, Gwynedd, on modern maps). No steeper public thoroughfare is named in the *Autocar-Motor Cycle* list of 128 'Famous Hills'. Long before the

BSA attack, it had been recognised as a notorious terror and had often figured in both car and motor-cycle demonstrations, but never previously had a manufacturer mounted such an all-embracing venture. Harry Perrey had the route accurately surveyed. It covered 0.66 miles and the gradient was found to vary from 1 in 20 to 1 in 2½ on the inside of the steepest of the six hairpins. The surface was loose shale, and on the day of the test it was dry.

Part of the plot was to make a fastest-time-of-the-day ascent on the ohv 350, specially prepared for the occasion, but the factory machine was not ready in time and a last-minute search for a substitute produced a completely standard model from the showroom stock of a Shrewsbury dealer.

To team with him, Perrey had chosen a young Daimler apprentice, G. G. Savage, and a Scots lad, G. McLean, who was on the BSA trials-riding strength. George Savage subsequently transferred to the Small Heath office staff and rose to head the company's motor-cycle sales force, a position he held when he retired in the 1960s. George McLean, after several years with BSA, became the leader of the almost invincible Douglas trials team, marrying another Douglas exponent, Louie Ball, who was then the supreme woman trials rider.

At Screw Hill, Perrey, Savage and McLean spent the best part of the day thrashing the various models up the gradient. The quickest solo ascent recorded by Vernon Brook's watch was that of George Savage on the ohv 350 — 1 min 53 sec, an average speed of 21.03 mph. And Perrey, with McLean as passenger, succeeded by dint of furiously exciting driving in hoisting the 1,000 cc outfit to the summit in 1 min 56 sec, only a whisker short of 21 mph.

After the official tests were over members of a large crowd of onlookers were invited to have a go, and the day ended with great jubilation, tinged only with the regret that it didn't count for Maudes Trophy recognition. *Motor Cycling* gave two well-illustrated, enthusiastic pages to the outing, but *The Motor Cycle* summarily, and rather stuffily, dismissed it as just another screwy stunt.

Within six weeks Perrey & Co were back in Wales with a much more ambitious project — a two-pronged assault on the 3,560 ft Snowdon Mountain. This majestic, snow-capped peak was not unfamiliar with motor vehicles; there had been some previous attempts by motor cyclists, and the record for the ascent was held by a 10 hp

BSA car which had taken 49 min 5 sec to cover the 4½ miles of rack-railway track. But Small Heath had learned a lesson on Screw Hill and when their party assembled at the Snowdon base camp, it included several ACU timekeepers and observers, headed by the Union's acting secretary, Major Gerald Dixon-Spain.

OC the factory contingent was Commander St John. The four riders were Harry Perrey, George McLean, George Savage and Harold Briggs. Among the helpers were Albert Wood, K. J. Davis, F. E. Thacker and a Mr Beale. Like Savage, Jim Davis was a salesman who could also ride; after many years with BSA he became a chief executive with a rival bicycle-building company. Ted Thacker was one of the competitions department's regular trials men, later achieving a considerable measure of fame as an Ariel trials teamster. Mr Beale was from the BSA accounts office: Small Heath were leaving nothing to chance!

There are several ways of reaching the summit of Snowdon. The two chosen for this venture were the rail route and a roughly parallel mountain path, both starting from Llanberis at an altitude of 373 ft and climbing in a south-easterly direction.

The first half-mile of the path consisted of gently rising metalled road through woodland, and then it degenerated into a narrow, 1 in 4 bank of rough stones, wet and slippery from a gushing stream. The second and third miles were of approximately 1 in 11 grade over shale and turf, and then it was all steep stuff, between 1 in 5 and 1 in 2½, for 1½ miles to the top. At 2,000 ft (third milestone) the lean air density caused engine power to fall off by 20 per cent. The path itself practically disappeared over the last half mile of projecting, ragged rocks.

On the railway track the riders were sometimes restricted to a narrow strip on the right side of the rails — so narrow that in places there was barely a foot of ground between the ends of the iron sleepers and a 1,000 ft precipice. For almost the whole of the route it was necessary to ride over the sleepers, which stood proud of the ballast by three to four inches. There were three sets of points, at the Hebron, Halfway and Clogwyn stations, that were particularly difficult to surmount.

As ill-luck would have it, the weather on the chosen day, May 14 1924, was appalling — high winds and heavy rain, and later almost impenetrable fog, combined to produce such forbidding conditions that it was not until 3.10 pm that Perrey, on an ohv 350 and McLean, aboard a side-valve 250 'Round Tank', bumped their way over the sleepers out of Llanberis station. At the same time Savage and Briggs, both on ohv 350s, departed from the nearby Victoria Hotel to tackle the pathway.

Well within an hour all four were together, 3,500 ft up in the clouds alongside the cairn that crowns Snowdonia.

Perrey, first up, and McLean, second, had made non-stop climbs in 24 min 6 sec and 30 min 38 sec respectively, without any kind of machine trouble.

Hardly had McLean stopped his engine than the crackle of an ohv came through the mist and George Savage joined the group, with a time of 41 min 8 sec. He had had a strenuous journey and at times had needed the help of the observers to keep going. Parts of the rocky track had been converted by the heavy rain into the beds of torrents, and the wet moss and grass slopes afforded no grip for the tyres.

Harold Briggs, owing to his heavier weight, had an even rougher passage and reached the top in an exhausted condition, having stopped his engine three times and taken a five-minute breather en route. His time, however, was well within the hour — 58 min 34 sec.

Apart from bent footrests and a bashed-in chaincase, there was nothing amiss with any of the machines and, indeed, on the following day in rather better weather, a second assault was made. The ACU party having departed, it could not be officially observed, but Jim Davis, riding the 'Round Tank' 250, made a spectacular climb of the mountain path in approximately 52 minutes. Verification was not possible because he reached the summit before the train that was carrying the observers!

On another 250, Ted Thacker had an exciting incident when he slipped from the path and fell 40 ft on to the railway below. The machine remained above and Ted, uninjured, soon scrambled up to remount and continue to the cairn. The two ohvs, which had been up the path the previous day, again made trouble-free climbs, there being, so *Motor Cycling* reported, 'no signs of falling off in power, nor, thanks to the Duralumin pushrods, any signs of slackness in the valve adjustment'.

But when the ACU came to judge the 1924 Maudes Trophy entries, they gave the prize to Nortons for a double End-to-End trek with a Big Four sidecar outfit that had averaged 20 mph for 4,000 miles, registering 68½ mpg.

In January 1925, BSA mounted a demonstration of a kind that had not hitherto been undertaken. Its purpose was to test the efficiency of the company's motor-cycle service organisation, and ACU observation was again in force, the Union nominating their newly appointed engineer, A. B. Bourne, to oversee the whole operation. A few years later Arthur Bourne joined *The Motor Cycle* and was its editor for a quarter of a century.

From a spare parts list, the bits and pieces needed to build a Model L 350 side-valve machine were ordered from 14 different stockists whose premises were scattered far and wide across England and Wales. They had no prior warning of the orders and were not subjected to any special urgency. Nevertheless, 44.11% of the dealers approached provided immediate over-the-counter supply; 15.73% delivered within 24 hours; 34.42% in 48 hours and 5.74% in 72 hours. A proportion of 2.67% of the items supplied were of the wrong type and had to be exchanged.

All the parts went to the ACU headquarters at 83 Pall Mall, London, where three assemblers built the machine in four hours, 44 minutes, using hand tools only. As soon as it was ready for the road, Arthur Bourne set out on a 104-mile course that included such well-known climbs as Succomb, Biggin, Pebblecombe and Reigate Hills. There were no involuntary stops and only one adjustment was needed, to the clutch lever, which was reset in 50 seconds.

Just in case it might be thought that this proof of BSA servicing was not sufficiently comprehensive, a similar test was carried out three months later, but this time the object was to show that, no matter how old an owner's mount might be, he could still rely on a supply of spares.

Again under ACU supervision, and using the same drill as before, all the parts were obtained within 72 hours from 16 agents to assemble an obsolete, 1914 557 cc machine. Harry Perrey rode it over the same 104-mile route and stopped involuntarily only once, to jury-rig a broken throttle cable.

Arthur Bourne was on the BSA scene again in January 1926 when he visited the Redditch works to chose at random a 350 ohv Super Sports machine from a batch of 20 identical mounts that were awaiting delivery. He rode it to Small Heath where it was mated with a sidecar built up from parts selected from stock. The complete outfit was given a brief run-in on the test track behind the factory.

22: *Dirt-track racing reached Britain from Australia in 1928 and many English motor-cycle makers produced machines for the cinders sport. This was the BSA type with which speedway's celebrated Jack Parker began his long reign as a world champion.*

23: *In its time there was no more stylish motor cycle than the BSA Model S 493 cc ohv Sloper. Introduced in 1926, it was steadily developed through many years. This 1929 edition has a two-port engine in an all-tube frame; later came the I-section 'backbone', a forged steel member replacing the tank rail.*

24: *From the time he joined the competitions department in 1926, until he retired in the 1960s, A. E. Perrigo was 'Mr BSA' to sporting motor cyclists. As a winner of countless awards, talent scout, team manager, technical adviser and factory executive, Bert's working life was a crusade for the high reputation of the Piled Arms. In this 1977 picture he is putting a shine on the silver helmet trophy he won at a Midlands grass-track meeting in 1927.*

B.S.A. 4.98 h.p. O.H.V. Vee-Twin
Model J35-12

£70

Price includes electric equipment and licence holder

Tax 45/-

25: *In the 1930s the War Office asked BSA for a medium weight V-twin for training purposes, and in 1934 a civilian version, the 498 cc ohv Model J-11, was marketed. Pictured is the 1935 J-12 type, costing £70 with electric equipment. A 750 cc Y-14 model followed within a year.*

B.S.A. 9.86 h.p Vee-Twin
Model G35-14

£75

Price includes electric equipment and licence holder

Tax 45/-

26: *Still going strong, the faithful old 986 cc big twin had, by 1935, been restyled as the Model G-14, with a new frame, detachable cylinder heads, enclosed valves, full electrical equipment and other modernities, all at £75.*

27: *A turning point in Small Heath engine design came with the 1938 Model M24. Revised by Val Page from the Empire Star pattern, it was the first machine to carry the Gold Star emblem and from it stemmed the legendary series of fast ohv singles that continued until 1962.*

28: *BSA engines were always thoroughly bench-tested. This view of the Armoury Road 'din house' shows, in the foreground, the then newly introduced 1937 B-type ohv units, with all-enclosed valve gear and dry-sump lubrication.*

29: *A department that is seldom seen by the customers is the drawing office. In this quiet room at Small Heath, designers' ideas were draughted into the working plans and tracings needed by the engineers to build the finished products.*

30: *In busy times the assembly lines in the Armoury Road plant could put together 2,000 motor cycles in a working week. Here a batch of 1937/38 ohv models are taking shape.*

31: *Knocking-off time in Armoury Road, 1935. Business was brisk; the slump was over; Hitler was just a nuisance; King George V was celebrating his Silver Jubilee — hence the bunting across the street.*

32: *Count them if you can! Automobile Association patrolmen taking delivery at Small Heath of a fleet of BSA box sidecar outfits in 1938. Before Mini-vans, Land-rovers and Relay, the AA's khaki-clad motor-cycle 'scouts' covered millions of miles operating their all-days, all-weather roadside repair and rescue service.*

33: *Left and right, The RTC's L/Cpl F. M. Rist and Sgt J. T. Dalby, British Army-entered riders in the 1938 International Six Days Trial. The NCOs rode BSAs and Fred Rist won a gold medal, starting him on a competitions career that led to stardom in the post-war years when he captained BSA's all-conquering team of trials and scrambles men.*

34: *A familiar steed for many thousands of Allied servicemen during World War 2 was the 500 cc side-valve Model M20. The machine on the right is a war veteran, that on the left is a recent rebuild, and both fig-ured in the Arnhem film,* A Bridge Too Far. *The picture was taken at Duxford Airfield in 1977.*

35: *First BSA to have a hyd-raulic telescopic front fork was the 1946 350 cc ohv Model B31, a type still regarded as one of Small Heath's 'best evers'. The machine shown is a 1953 model, for which plunger rear suspension was an optional extra.*

36: Motor Cycling's *reporting team for the 1947 Scottish Six Days Trial 'weigh-in' on the waterfront at Fort William. Left to right, Bob Holliday (BSA A7 twin), Graham Walker (Norton) and Mrs Holliday (BSA 4-cylinder three-wheeler).*

37: *The immortal BSA D1 Bantam 125 cc two-stroke, as it arrived in 1948, with a rigid frame and undamped teles. It quickly grew plunger rear suspension, was consistently updated and uprated, and remained in production for some 20 years.*

38: *For hard work and light running costs it was difficult to outpoint BSA's post-war 250 cc side-valve C10 models, which went through many stages of development following this early example with Bantam-type teles and plunger suspension.*

39: *A new frame layout, with a pivoted rear fork controlled by adjustable spring units, was introduced in the mid-1950s to carry the 500 cc enclosed-ohv B33 engines. Full-width hubs and revised, compact gearboxes were further features.*

40: *By 1954 swinging fork rear suspension was either standard or optional equipment for most of the BSA range. Applied to the 650 cc A10 Golden Flash vertical twin model it added super comfort to the attributes of as handsome a motor cycle as ever came from Small Heath.*

41: *BSA's post-war sidecar star, Harold Tozer, retired from competitions after winning the British Experts Trial (for the second time) in 1952. Here he occupies his own sidecar while Bob Holliday tries to emulate the maestro's tactics on the notorious Cotswold horror, Hodgecombe Hill.*

42: *In trials, scrambles and moto-cross, all around the world for nearly 20 years on BSAs, Jeff Smith was always 'the man most likely' to win. From 1953 until the closure of the Armoury Road competitions department in 1971, he loyally rode the Piled Arms marque to countless victories.*

43: *As a serving officer, Captain W. E. Dow had achieved a trials riding reputation on BSAs in International Six Days events before he went racing on Gold Stars in the Clubman's TT and in long distance grands prix. Here he is on the Goldie with which he won the 1955 Senior Clubman's.*

On the next day, January 27, Perrey, with Bourne as passenger, took the outfit to mid-Wales, reaching the Buckley Arms Hotel, Dinas Mawddwy, in time for lunch. In the afternoon they drove to Bwlch-y-Groes (Pass of the Cross), a notorious test grade of even greater severity than Screw Hill. Whereas the latter was short and sharp, 'the Bwlch' involved a 1.57-mile climb, commencing with a 1 in 4 hairpin and having an average gradient of 1 in 6, rising to 1,250 ft. From the summit, the track winds down into Bala with, on fine days, superb views of distant Snowdonia.

After Perrey had made a few tentative ascents, George McLean, who was acting as reserve driver, in charge of petrol and other supplies, checked adjustments and changed the sparking plug. Everything was then ready for a target of 60 climbs — a till-then record for the hill.

On the following day 40 consecutive ascents were made without trouble, and in the evening McLean reset the inlet tappet and fitted a new plug. The remaining 20 climbs were made on the next day, under hailstorm conditions, but the outfit ran perfectly and Perrey blasted up for the last time in 4 min 20 sec, over 20 mph. Timekeeper Vernon Brook calculated that in the course of the test the BSA had scaled the equivalent of some 65,000 feet — nearly 13 miles.

To show that no 'special skill' was needed, a 61st ascent was bravely made by Commander Herbert, with Joe Bryan in the sidecar. After a faultless performance, they arrived back at the 'Buckley Arms' soaked through and eager for the celebrations. The Commander had not ridden a motor cycle for four years.

Chapter 9

The vintage era

'. . . of good and rare quality' — *New English Dictionary*

Since its formation in 1946, the Vintage Motor Cycle Club, nowadays with a membership exceeding 4,000, has been the ruling authority on all matters concerning the collection, preservation and exhibition — both static and mobile — of bygone makes of machines. The club decided at its inaugural meeting that a distinction should be made between the 'genuine antiques' and the models that flourished in the halcyon years of the inter-World Wars period. A Veteran motor cycle, it was decreed, was one manufactured before January 1 1915; Vintage mounts were those made between that date and December 31 1930. And it was in the latter part of the Vintage era that the motor-cycle movement grew into a boom. In 1926 the number of machines in use in Britain was 636,771, an increase over the previous year of 65,417. Up to the end of the decade the annual registration figures continued to rise, reaching 731,298 in 1929, a high-water mark that was not to be overtaken until 1950.

Rivalry between the factories was intense. The two leading Birmingham companies, BSA and Ariel, at times achieved outputs that topped 2,000 units a week, but profits were not great, for the whole industry was fighting a price-cutting war that had been started by the incredibly cheap 500 cc Model P Triumph (£42 17s 6d in 1925) and the 350 cc EW Douglas (£41 10s in 1926). Small Heath's best buy was still the 250 side-valver which by then had been marked down to only £36 10s.

As always happens when giants join battle, smaller fry get knocked about, and many of the old-established, but precariously financed, motor-cycle firms were unable to compete, either closing their doors or transferring to other fields of business. Among those that suffered was the Bordesley Engineering Co Ltd, of Aston, which had been making reliable and well-liked Connaught machines since 1910. Its demise, among so many others, would not have been particularly remarkable but for the fact that it brought into prominence a man who was to have a leading part in the development of BSA fortunes, especially in the realms of the sport.

The name of Albert E. Perrigo first appeared in the technical press when, driving a Connaught sidecar outfit in the 1926 Victory Trial, he won a silver medal. Although he was later often referred to by ill-informed journalists as 'the well-known Italian rider', Bert Perrigo's antecedents were rooted in the heart of Birmingham where his family owned a bakery business. Doing the bread delivery rounds on a box-sidecar combination had spurred his interest in motor cycles and in 1924 he had joined the Connaught firm, on whose two-stroke machines he began to show his neat, precise style as a trials rider. It so happened that, just as the Connaught concern was beginning to fold up, Harry Perrey transferred from BSA to Ariel, and in July 1926 Bert moved to the competitions department at Small Heath, becoming, as the years rolled on, not only a pre-eminent playing captain of the company's trials teams but also a valuable executive on the commercial side of their activities.

At this period reliability trials were important items in the propaganda budgets of the major manufacturers and it is worth taking a look at the situation as it stood around 1927. The semi-sporting type of event, as exemplified by the Motor Cycling Club's long-distance classics, the London-Land's End and London-Edinburgh runs, and the 24-hour stints such as the Birmingham-Holyhead trial, though still popular with private owners, were losing support from the trade which favoured the growing numbers of one-day open trials (ie, open to riders from all the ACU-affiliated clubs.) The grandfather of these was the Colmore Cup Trial, first organised by the Sutton Coldfield and N Birmingham Automobile Club in 1911. Next in importance was the Victory Trial, instituted in 1919 by the Birmingham Motor Cycle Club to commemorate the end of World War I.

There were many others, so many, in fact, that there came a time when only a selected dozen or so were approved for participation by factory-entered competitors. In this trade-supported category were always those two marathon enduros, the International and the Scottish Six Days Trials. Strictly for the trade only was the ACU's Six Days Stock Machine Trial in which works teams competed on standard-specification models. Scrambling, forerunner of moto-cross and popularised by the Scott Trial, was only just beginning to make headway, and 'knobbly' tyres were still to come.

All the big companies, notably AJS, Ariel, BSA, Douglas, Matchless, New Imperial, Norton, Royal Enfield, Rudge, Sunbeam and Velocette, in addition to entering their own staff men, signed on the freelance talent as it showed itself among the privateers. Competitions departments, hitherto combined with the experimental engineers' 'din houses', became separate workshops, staffed by the firm's best mechanics and fitters, with high-priority rights to draw on the components stores and to have special items fabricated in the factory.

A glance at the entry list for the 1927 Colmore Cup reveals an extraordinary variety of personalities; all kinds of people were anxious to have a go — managing directors, designers, department chiefs, road racers, road testers, professional trialsmen, factory-backed part-timers and enthusiastic amateurs, they all mixed happily together with determination to bring credit to their own particular marques.

Bert Perrigo found himself heading a BSA squad that included Jack Amott, a technician-rider of vast experience that extended to the Isle of Man TT; Phil Cranmore, a Birmingham dealer who had won the Colmore in 1925 on a Zenith and became the outright winner in 1926 aboard Harry Perrey's 350 cc BSA combination; Jack Humphries, one of BSA's most seasoned soloists; Jack Parker, just getting launched on a riding career that was to make him one of the all-time greats on the speedway circuits; John Lloyd, who also took to the cinders but was then a Birmingham University undergraduate reading medicine; the Debenham sisters; Cyril and Muriel Lord, a consistently successful trials pair; and those two veteran experts in the big-twin sidecar class, Bertie Bird and Howard Uzzell.

Across the city at Selly Oak, Harry Perrey's troupe of Arielists numbered design-technician Cecil Booker, assembly-shop manager Billy Woodcock, road-tester Eric Eschborn, staff trialsman Geoff Proe and amateur gentleman Peter Chamberlain. Scion of the political family, grandson of Midland Bank chairman Sir James Smith and nephew of BSA director Sir Hallewell Rogers, Peter was then on the verge of his fame as a motor-cycling journalist and ACU committeeman.

For the record, the Cup was won that year by Birmingham's sidecar-driving Sunbeam dealer, Alan Watson. And a month later a solo Sunbeam took the Victory Trial prize, ridden by the famous speedster, George Dance.

It was about this time that a spate of Round-the-World adventures set in. In December 1926 a pair of Frenchmen, Sexé and Andrieu, had completed a global tour on Gillet solos. Almost concurrently, an American couple, Mr and Mrs Ballard, arrived in England, also on a circumnavigational course. They bought a New Hudson combination and disappeared eastwards. How they fared seems never to have been reported in British papers. In February 1927 D. R. Hall departed on an HRD outfit, taking a wager to beat the Frenchmen's time of five months and three weeks. Research has uncovered no mention of what happened to him, either, but another charioteer pair, John Gill and Captain Geoffrey Malins, with an OEC-Temple outfit reached Australia where Malins surrendered his place in the sidecar to a Melbourne enthusiast, P. E. Irving. Thus did Phil 'Slide Rule' Irving reach England to embark on his career as a motor-cycle designer.

There was nothing of a Jules Verne-like urgency about BSA's entry into terrestrial touring. Two 986 cc twins were prepared with box sidecars carrying a welter of equipment. The drivers were B. H. Cathrick and J. P. Castley, and they left Small Heath in September 1927. Bertram Cathrick was an experienced, much-travelled, 26-year-old BSA agent from Pierce-bridge, near Darlington; back in 1922 he had won a special first-class award in the Scottish Six Days trial and later worked on a rubber plantation in the Malay States. Somewhat younger, John Castley was a member of the editorial staff of *The Motor Cycle*.

Their object was not only to circle the earth but also to spread the 'British is best' gospel as widely as possible. They were in no great hurry, but nevertheless they passed through 24 countries in the course of 19 months, crossed the Sahara and the Andes and were back in March 1928 at Southampton, being feted in London on the following day at a Savoy Hotel luncheon hosted by Godfrey Herbert and Joe Bryan. Neither of the machines had needed anything more than regular maintenance in 25,000 miles, and they brought back valuable information on export-market possibilities and conditions.

With the September announcement of the 1928 range, BSA introduced a two-stroke model. It was not, in fact, the first stroker they had ever made for, five years earlier, they had experimented with a 200 cc machine of that type, but the project had not come up to expectations and was abandoned.

Catalogued as the Model A28, the little newcomer had a simple, three-port 60 × 61.5 mm, 174 cc, upright engine with an overhung crank in a case containing a two-speed arrangement consisting of pairs of spur gears selected by dog-clutches. The unit, which ran 'backwards', was mounted in a cradle frame of straight, bolted-up tubes, there being no lugs or brazed joints. At £28 10s it was well received.

The other mounts in the programme were the B-type de luxe (three-speed) 250 side valve; L-type 350 side valve, light ohv and super sports ohv; S-type 493 side valve standard and de luxe and ohv (Sloper); H-type 557 side valve; E-type 770 light and de luxe twins; G-type 986 standard and Colonial twins — 13 different machines. Hardly any specification changes had been made, except that the 350 super sports now had a cylinder head similar to that of the Sloper.

Held early in 1928, in the Cotswolds, the Stock Trial saw the BSA team of Perrigo, Humphries, Parker and Uzzell all gold-medal winners, the only other makers whose men had lost no marks being Matchless, Rudge and Sunbeam. The Rudge sidecar outfit, driven by the company's competitions manager, Geoffrey Butcher, was undoubtedly as per catalogue but, in some mysterious manner unknown to the ACU, it possessed an urge that was way above a 'stock' performance, as I soon found out when I acquired it immediately after the trial. That it had been assembled by Jack Amott, who had moved to Rudge-Whitworth, probably had something to do with it.

No sooner was the Stock Trial over than Bert Perrigo set off on one of the medal-winning 493 cc machines, having been handed a £1 note and instructed to travel as far as he could on the money. He covered 1,670 miles on 18½ gallons of petrol and 1¼ pints of oil — averages of 90 and 10,700 mpg. Petrol, about that time, could be had for as little as a shilling a gallon, for the government tax, first imposed in 1910 (3d per gallon) had been discontinued after World War I and was not reintroduced until 1929.

Despite soaring sales graphs, there was little joy for BSA shareholders. In April 1928 the company, which, with its £5,000,000 capital and ownership of the Daimler concern, was one of the largest in the motor industry, published its balance sheet, summarised by *The Motor* as follows:

'On last year's trading, the balance to credit on profit and loss account amounts to £202,063 0s 2d which, with the amount brought forward from the last account, provides the sum of £491,776 3s 5d, about £50,000 more than was available for distribution the previous year. While the dividends on the 5% and 6% preference shares and the interest on the 6½% 12-year notes are paid, it is not proposed to pay a dividend on the ordinary shares, but to carry forward a balance of £336,822 6s 7d. A dividend of 5% on the ordinary shares would absorb £109,086 18s 4d. This was paid in 1925, and in 1926 a dividend of 6% was declared'.

A month later the company said they were using the carry-forward sum to wipe out, in part, the 6½% 12-year-old notes issued in 1920, for which purpose an issue was being made of £2,000,000 6% first-mortgage debenture stock at 98%. Notice was given that the 6½% notes would be redeemed by July 1 1928.

Before the year was out BSA had added to their coffers the proceeds of the sale of the old Lodge Road, Redditch factory, transferring all the motor-cycle and cycle component shops to Small Heath. Albert Eadie, who had founded the Redditch plant, relinquished his BSA directorship for health reasons; he died two years later.

Saddle tanks were coming into fashion and for their 1929 range BSA had them on all their models except the 986 cc twin, which was now listed as the WT type in recognition of the World Tour. The 174 cc two-stroke and 249 cc side-valve bikes were continued with few other changes. The 349 cc group had vertical side- and overhead-valve engines and an ohv Sloper; the same theme applied in the 493 cc bracket, to which was added a side-valve Sloper; the trusty old 557 cc mount also had its side-valve engine tilted forward.

Works-tuned versions of the 493 cc Slopers were made available — for an extra £5 they had special cams and high-compression pistons. After complaints from dealers that, outwardly, they were hard to distinguish from their staider brethren, the factory marked their timing cases with stencilled-on red stars. This seemingly unremarkable afterthought was, quite by accident, to lead to the naming of the celebrated Star series of machines, about which there is much to come in later chapters.

From America, via Australia, the sport of dirt-track racing had come to Britain in 1928, and initially Douglas and Rudge machines were predominantly successful on the quarter-mile circuits. But at Olympia in 1929 a dozen or more makers were on the band waggon, among them

BSA who, largely through Jack Parker's efforts, had developed the Sloper into one of the most powerful contemporary cinder-shifters.

However, John Lloyd was not satisfied that he was getting the utmost from the Sloper he was using, courtesy of his sponsor, Phil Cranmore. As a medical student, John reckoned he knew something about alcohol and he prescribed himself a formula for a potent 'dope' fuel, which he had made up by a wholesale chemist, secretly exchanging the brew for his normal spirit. That Saturday night at the Perry Barr Stadium we watched John slide through his heats with the greatest of ease, and when he came into the paddock after winning the final he could not resist telling Cranmore the valuable secret of his success. But Phil, himself well versed in the wiles of motor-cycle competitions, showed no elation. 'I thought your tank had a funny smell,' he said, 'so I emptied it before the meeting. You were running on straight Discol!'

∗   ∗   ∗

On a brisk November morning in 1929 I passed the guardhouse in Armoury Road, to be greeted by a cheery young Scot, D. W. Munro, one of the backroom boys in the technical developments department. He had been deputed to introduce me to BSA's latest line in transport — a little 8.9 hp three-wheeled, two-seater car. Being an Aero Morgan addict myself, I thought it looked a bit chunky and top-heavy but, after David Munro and I had spent the day chuntering along Warwickshire by-roads and romping up grades like Sunrising and Edge Hills, I was completely sold by the way in which so much punchy power had been combined with good springing, sure road-holding and a high degree of occupant-comfort. It even had a proper hood and side curtains, and the whole thing weighed under 8 cwt, the legal limit for an annual tax of £4.

From the ingenious minds of Freddie Hulse and Harold Briggs, the original BSA three-wheeler had an engine that obviously owed ancestry to the Hotchkiss type that had powered the 10 hp car. The 90 degree transverse V-twin, ohv, air-cooled unit had dimensions of 85 × 90 mm, 1,021.5 cc. On the forward end of the crankshaft was a cork-insert centre-plate clutch with a toothed flywheel for a Bendix-type starter motor. Farther forward was a three-speed and reverse crash gearbox, operation of which was by a remote-control linkage that, having to bypass the right-side cylinder, brought the long, stalky gearlever up through the floorboards between the brake and accelerator pedals. Ahead of the box was a worm-driven, planetary spur-gear differential, the worm-wheel also carrying the drum for the front brake.

From each side of the diff projected short shafts, on which were flexible fabric couplings, and from these Cardan shafts splined into the hub units containing simple Hookes-pattern universal joints. The stub-axle components were carried, top and bottom, between transverse quarter-elliptic leaf springs, four on each side, anchored inboard above and below the diff case. The springs took all the driving and braking forces for there was no other provision for countering torque reactions. The layout was straightforward, neat and inexpensive, and it worked very well, although it could produce surprises for the uninitiated. For example, severe braking on a slippery surface could result in one front wheel locking and the other revolving backwards! This was a characteristic of transmission brakes working through a differential, and older readers may remember how the phenomenon occurred when London's Unic taxis tried to stop on wet wood-block paving.

Another disconcerting trait manifested itself when the front wheels were turned towards full lock. With a Hookes joint, any variation from a straight-through drive results in a 'slow-quick-slow' rotation of the driven shaft, the effect increasing with the angle of deviation. In normal use this was barely noticeable with the three-wheeler, but on a tight hairpin bend the erratic behaviour of the inner wheel could be quite startling. The true constant-velocity joint that solves the problem on modern fwd cars had not then been developed for vehicle use.

The BSA chassis consisted of channel-section members on each side of the power unit and a central, tubular backbone between light-section girders supporting the body. The large-diameter tube ended in a trunnion in which was pivoted the forged-steel arm carrying the rear axle. From the forward end of the swinging arm a quarter-elliptic spring worked inside the backbone. A brace and jack were the only tools needed to change the wheels around. A rear drum brake was linked to the pedal and could also be independently applied by a lever that had to be pushed forward to the 'on' position.

Bodywork was of the then fashionable 'fabric' style, ie, leather-cloth stretched over a wood framework. Inflatable rubber cushions were used, and mending seat punctures was routine maintenance.

Starting up could be difficult. The six-volt battery, necessarily a lightweight, needed to be in tip-top condition to spin a stone-cold engine. A heavy-duty, detachable handle, that poked through the dummy radiator, was a vital item of equipment, but swinging a 1,000 cc twin fast enough to strike a light was hard work, not eased by the fact that the Solex carburettor was remotely located high up between the cylinders, and the inlet tracts were long pipes curving into the ports like the horns of a water buffalo. But, once going, the twin was a lively lad, with a more rumbustious, though less comfortable, performance than the aluminium-bodied, water-cooled, side-valve four-cylinder model that came later and which was the basis of the very popular and handsome little BSA Scout sports car.

I drove my twin- and four-cylinder trikes over many thousands of miles, never had any major breakdowns and was never threatened with the overturning tendancy that was snidely said by some to haunt the type. Indeed, if the water-cooled model, sensibly updated, was available today, I could easily be persuaded . . .

*   *   *

It was in the same November of 1929 that the Birmingham Club staged the first British Experts Trial. Conceived by the period's ace rider, Graham Goodman, it was planned as the ultimate sorter-outer of the *crème de la crème* of trialsmen. Open only to those who had won premier and capacity-class awards in the major events of the year, it was deliberately made tough. Goodman, who never himself competed, worked like a Trojan to discover new terror hills and sections, and to perfect the standards of organisation and observation. From the beginning, it received the maximum possible support from those who were fortunate to be eligible and its prestige continues undiminished to the present day. Graham's prime aim was that it should pinpoint only two competitors — the supreme experts in the solo and sidecar classes. First to receive those accolades were Bert Perrigo (349 BSA) and Dennis Mansell (490 Norton).

*   *   *

The success of the BSA Sloper had brought about a rash of inclined engines and two-port cylinder heads: and dry-sump lubrication was superseding the total-loss system. At the Show a huge variety of machine types was available, as indicated by the Small Heath range of 18 basic models listed for 1930. At the lower end of the scale the 174 cc two-stroke had a three-speed brother; at the top were the 986 cc twins and the three-wheeler.

In the mid-range bracket were some entirely new, or adapted, models designed to meet a promised concession to be introduced by the Chancellor of the Exchequer, Winston Churchill, raising the 30 shillings per annum tax class from a weight limit of 200 lb to 224 lb. But a sudden change of Government brought a system whereby machines were to be taxed at 5% of their cost. The whole industry, which had spent a great deal of money and thought on devising mounts that weighed under 224 lb (some of which were up to 500 cc) protested violently that its efforts had been wasted. Eventually, although not until July 1930, the 224 lb limit was conceded — but too late to catch the sales season for that year.

At 170 lb, the 250 Round Tank and its derivatives had come well within the former 200 lb class, but after a production run of over 35,000 units — of which a large proportion went to the Post Office for use by telegram delivery boys — the type was discontinued and replaced by an entirely new design of quarter-litre, the duplex-cradle-frame side-valve B30-3 model, specifically intended to fit into the 224 lb class, and costing £37 10s. There was also a snappy ohv version (B30-4) and a new side-valve 350 (L30-5), both the latter machines qualifying for the weight limit if fitted with acetylene gas, instead of electric lights, The Sloper, now designated the S30-13, had a chrome-plated tank and the frame embodied an I-section drop-forged backbone-cum-steering head in place of top tubes and tank rails. The two-strokes, 250s, sv 350 and sv and ohv light-engined 493 models had upright cylinders; all the other singles had Sloper characteristics and two-port heads for the ohv types.

All through 1930 the BSA trials riders kept up the pressure. Perrigo was best soloist in the Victory, and Cranmore best sidecar driver in the Scottish Six Days. There was a flutter of protest when it was learned that the ACU had not given Marjorie Cottle her usual place in Britain's all-ladies Silver Vase team for the International Six Days. Her new 249 cc BSA, it was said, was not powerful enough. Marjorie, a much-experienced and consistently successful rider, wiped the eyes of the Pall Mall pundits by winning a gold medal for a fault-free performance.

When the new season's range was paraded in September it had been pruned down to 12 motor cycles, plus three editions of the three-wheeler, now offered in one form as a four-seater. Gone were the two-strokes, the Colonial twin and several of the mid-range types. There was one completely new machine, an upright-engined ohv 350 with a stiffened version of the 250's duplex frame. Prices had been cut, but Parkerising and cadmium plating had been introduced to give a better finish and longer life to frames and cycle parts. The larger machines had handlebar-mounted instrument and switch panels, embellishments much in vogue that year.

As any of these machines, if made before the end of 1930, qualify for Vintage approval, here is the list, in type order. Models 1, 2 and 4 were in the 30 shillings tax class; all the singles had vertical engines except the H and S types:

		£	s
B31-1	249 sv	37	10
B31-2	249 ohv	40	0
B31-3	249 ohv de lux	42	0
L31-4	349 sv	38	10
L31-5	349 sv de luxe	42	0
L31-6	349 ohv de luxe	45	0
S31-7	493 sv	47	10
H31-8	557 sv de luxe	52	0
S31-9	493 ohv	52	0
S31-10	493 ohv de luxe	56	0
E31-11	770 sv twin	58	0
G31-12	986 sv twin	69	0
Three-wheeler 1021 sports		125	0
Three-wheeler 1021 sports de luxe		125	0
Three-wheeler 1021 sports family		127	0

So ended the Vintage epoch. With its passing came compulsory third-party insurance, abolition of the 20 mph general speed limit (in force since 1903), large-size rear number plates for motor cycles, strict pillion-seat rules, the banning of side-saddle riding, the raising of the minimum age for a driving licence from 14 to 16.

And a world-wide slump.

Chapter 10

De profundis

Per aspera ad astra *(by rough roads to the stars)*

The collapse of the American stock market — the devastating Wall Street crash of 1929 — had its impact on Great Britain and the European continent generally in the early 1930s, the years of hunger marches, dole queues and abysmal depression. The British motor-cycle industry, never really financially stable and always vitally exposed to the winds of change, was hit hard. Its plight was partly due to its own indecision as to the role it was trying to play in the world of wheels: was motor cycling a sport, a hobby or a viable form of personal transport? Nobody ever seemed sure, and the conundrum has remained unresolved to this day. With a few exceptions, notably individualist George Brough, most manufacturers, in their various ways, sought to cater for all tastes, offering widely diverse ranges and constantly altering and updating specifications. This process was wastefully expensive both for the firms and for their agents, who were compelled to lock up capital in multitudes of spare parts. Henry Ford's recipe for success — one model only, in any colour provided that it was black — went unheeded.

Britain's motor-cycle makers exploited every dodge they could think of to keep afloat. Some merged, amalgamated or otherwise reconstructed their companies. A few, like Triumph, Ariel and Raleigh, plunged into the light car and trade delivery vehicle fields. Others, such as Humber and New Hudson, abandoned motor cycles altogether. AJS went even farther afield, making cars, lorries and radio sets. But, despite everything, the famous Wolverhampton marque was one of the first of the major motor-cycle firms to succumb to the Great Depression, going into liquidation in 1931. There were rumours that BSA would acquire the business and, indeed, Joe Bryan, by this time sales manager of BSA Cycles, admitted that 'negotiations are in train'. However, the Collier brothers of Woolwich eventually took over AJS, combining it with their Matchless operation to form Associated Motor Cycles Ltd.

There were some bright patches amid the gloom. One was a resurgence of popularity for bicycles, and BSA, Raleigh and Hercules fought a stern battle for the lion's share of this welcome market. Three-wheelers were also in demand, and Ministry of Transport figures published in September 1931 showed 12,371 such vehicles in use as against 11,568 the year before. Small Heath had helped in this direction by reducing the price of the de luxe and sports V-twin models to £100. At the same time it was revealed that the Post Office had 2,000 motor cycles in use, 90 per cent of them BSAs, and BSA machines were being used by police authorities in 22 counties and 36 boroughs.

Rather strangely, in view of the hard times, motor-cycle sport flourished with unabated enthusiasm. Although the ACU Stock Machine Trial had had to be abandoned through lack of entries, there was plenty of support for the TT and the Continental Grands Prix. Also, reliability trials attracted such a large following that it was sometimes necessary to make mid-week fixtures for important events in order to avoid duplications on Saturdays.

As they had done in 1926, BSA decided not to take stand space at the 1931 show but, at their customary dealers' private show, they had a well-selected range of 12 solo types for 1932 that included two new 499 cc (85 × 88 mm) models, detachable cylinder heads for the side-valvers, coupled brakes and a redesigned four-speed, foot-controlled gearbox for the sports types. In the 224 lb-tax class there were 250 and 350 ohv models and a 350 sv. The medium-weight group offered standard and de luxe ohvs, an sv and a new sports machine, the L32-5 Blue Star — all of 349 cc, with four-speed boxes, upright engines and forged-steel backbone frames. Also with vertical engines were the three W models — a 499 cc sv, a standard ohv version and a sports Blue Star edition. The only Slopers were the 493 cc ohv de luxe S32-8 and its 557 cc sv counterpart, the H32-9, both with qd wheels. Still in harness was the 986 cc WT big twin.

The new Blue Stars, which carried their distinguishing enamelled emblems on the timing cases, were the work of designer Herbert Perkins, who had given them high-compression pistons, double-coil valve springs, special cams, pump-type Amal carburettors, high-level exhaust pipes and positive-stop gear control. In addition to the resultant high performance, the Blue Stars had frame changes that greatly improved steering qualities. After Bert Perrigo had won a gold medal on the 500 cc prototype as a British Trophy team member in the International Six Days Trial, had won the West of England trial and had become the solo British Expert aboard a 350 model, Blue Stars were well and truly launched as desirable property for fast tourists and sporting clubmen, of which latter there were rapidly increasing numbers. Notwithstanding the difficulties of the times, the ACU was able to claim at the end of 1931 that it had over 400 affiliated clubs — a record.

Nevertheless, the overall trading situation was becoming more and more serious. The Olympia Show was so poorly supported, by both the industry and the public, that the Manufacturers' Union decided not to hold the exhibition in 1932.

Then, as the national economy struggled to recover its equilibrium, the motor-cycle industry also glimpsed light at the end of the tunnel. Sales of new machines began to pick up, although many riders could only afford to licence their mounts on a part-yearly basis, laying them up during the winter and emerging like Easter lilies in the spring. Unable to meet the expense of car ownership, family men bought three-wheelers and sidecar combinations, there being a large increase in the ranks of sidecar makers at this time. And there was no holding back of enthusiasm for the sport. One example of the keen spirit prevailing is seen in the formation, in March 1932, of the Brands Hatch Combine, a consortium of four south-east London clubs which made an arrangement with a Kentish landowner and raised £1,000 for equipping a three-quarter-mile grass track at Farningham.

In that year's Victory Trial Perrigo was the best soloist and with John Humphries and Fred Povey, all on Blue Stars; BSA took the team prize. In the Sunbeam Club's London-to-Brighton Pioneer Run, speedway expert Squib Burton rode a 240 cc BSA-Minerva, circa 1902, and got a finisher's plaque.

Over a difficult course centred on Merano, Italy, Great Britain's ISDT team succeeded, after two consecutive years of failure, in recapturing the Trophy, Perrigo (Blue Star), George Rowley (AJS) and Peter Bradley (Sunbeam and sidecar) triumphing over the home-side Gilera trio in the final speed test. Britain also won the Silver Vase contest and the ever-present Marjorie Cottle took her 250 BSA through to win another gold medal.

As there was no Olympia, a number of manufacturers organised their own exhibitions of their new season's ranges. BSA staged theirs at Small Heath, inviting the public as well as dealers to inspect the 1933 machines, with chairman of the Birmingham Small Arms parent company, A. H. Potter, as host. Godfrey Herbert, BSA Cycles Ltd managing director, unveiling a four-cylinder version of the three-wheeler, said that 50 per cent of 'tricycles' registered in the past year were BSAs, and that the company's share of the motor-cycle market had not only been maintained but the whole output of 1932 machines had been sold, so there would be no clearance lines.

To keep the four-cylinder 'trike' within the 8 cwt, £4 annual tax limit BSA engineers had performed wonders. The 1,074 cc (60 × 95 mm) water-cooled, side-valve iron cylinder block had an aluminium head with 14 mm plugs; the gearbox, clutch housing and worm-drive casing were cast in Elektron alloy; and the body, slightly wider and longer than that of the twin types, was panelled in aluminium. To give a more sporting profile, the rear suspension arm was curved to allow a lower pivot point. Maximum speed was 65 mph and the price £125. The twin range continued in five styles, ranging from the standard fabric-bodied model at £100 to the super-sports version with aluminium coachwork at £115.

A revised method of taxation, to become effective from June 1 1933, had brought about changes in the solo machine programme. The 224 lb-weight class was discarded and instead there was a three-tier system based solely on cubic capacity, viz, under 150 cc remained at 15s per annum; 150-250 cc was set at 30s; and over 350 cc, the duty was £3. This meant that 250 cc mounts, no longer labouring under an arbitrary weight restriction, had received considerable attention and development.

Announcing their programme in September, in anticipation of the new tax rules, BSA dropped the 224 lb 350 cc sv and ohv models and substituted two new 250s — the only models in the 13-machine range sold with electric lighting (Maglita) as standard equipment. On all the others Magdyno instruments were offered as optional extras.

The new 249 cc models were identical except that one (B33-1, £32) was a side-valve and the other (B33-2, £34) was an ohv single-port with exposed pushrods and plain-bearing rockers mounted on bolted-on plates. A simple loop frame carried the engines and three-speed gearboxes.

A third, more elaborate, 250 was the Blue Star Junior (B33-3), which had a high-compression piston, two-port head, special cams and valve springs, pushrod return springs, a duplex-tube frame, steering damper, hand-adjustable shock absorbers, high-level pipes and foot-control for the four-speed gearbox. Its price was £44.

The two 350s were altered in both bore and stroke, being now 71 × 88 mm, 349 cc, and had redesigned cylinder heads. The standard type R33-4 cost £45, and an extra £2 10s bought the R33-5 Blue Star with equipment similar to that of its Junior brother. Hardly any changes were made to the 499 cc W33-6 sv, the W33-7 standard ohv or the W33-8 Blue Star, but a new 500, based on Perrigo's ISDT mount, was introduced as the W33-9 Special, at £60.

The Special had a slipper piston with a compression ratio of 7½:1, polished ports, a large-bore TT Amal carburettor and a Lucas racing magneto. The high-level exhaust system was not available for this model but the pipes were arranged to be of the correct length for racing when the tubular silencers were removed. Like

the 350 and 500 Blue Stars, it had finned pipe nuts with a cross-brace.

The only Slopers left in the range were the models M33-10 and 11, respectively sv and ohv types with revised bore and stroke measurements of 85 × 105 mm, 595 cc. A light edition of the 986 cc twin was produced as a dual-purpose machine for solo or sidecar work. In a shortened frame, this G33-12 had a high-compression engine with improved valve gear and new cams; the four-speed box had combined hand and foot operation. The WT model was continued, practically unaltered.

The production-racer nature of the new 500 Special was an indication that Small Heath policy towards track work was undergoing a change, but the firm had allowed this branch of the sport to become the special province of Norton, Rudge, Velocette and Excelsor, and BSAs rarely figured in race results. Indeed, it was a standard 350 Blue Star sidecar outfit, owned by Brooklands exponent J. J. Hall, that brought the marque back into the Weybridge picture when P. Brewster, E. A. Dussek and W. M. Couper shared the work of breaking the Double 12-Hour

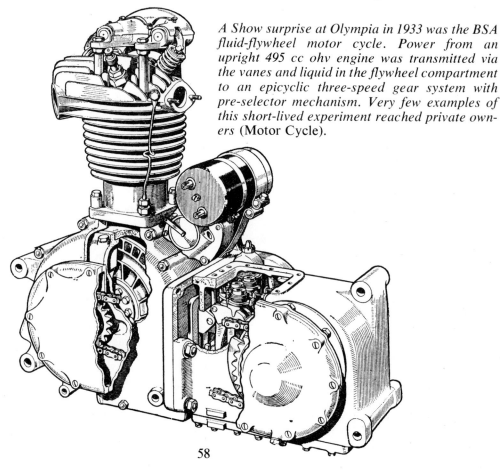

A Show surprise at Olympia in 1933 was the BSA fluid-flywheel motor cycle. Power from an upright 495 cc ohv engine was transmitted via the vanes and liquid in the flywheel compartment to an epicyclic three-speed gear system with pre-selector mechanism. Very few examples of this short-lived experiment reached private owners (Motor Cycle).

Class B/S record in October 1932, 19 years after Kenneth Holden's 1913 five-mile success recorded in Chapter 3. Jim Hall's machine covered 1,029 miles, 491 yards, averaging 42.88 mph despite numerous delays caused by gearbox and sidecar chassis repairs. The old record, held by a Douglas outfit, had stood since 1922. During the dark hours the BSA was shown the way by the headlamps of Mike Couper's following Lagonda, a make of car with which he was to become celebrated in the world of motoring sport.

As the year closed a new BSA star appeared among the trialsmen when H. J. Flook made the best sidecar performance in the British Experts event. Harold Flook, usually with his wife as passenger, had begun his long-lasting run of successes that included membership of the British Trophy team in the ISDT.

On a 500 Special, Fred Povey won the 1933 Victory Trial and Bert Perrigo made best solo performance in the Cotswold Cups with a 350 Blue Star. In the Experts event Povey was best soloist and Flook again showed his superiority in the sidecar category.

Olympia reopened with a bang in November 1933, BSA signalling their return to the old glass-roofed hall in Kensington with a dazzling display of more than 60 machines — solos, sidecars and three-wheelers, in a multiplicity of colour schemes and alternative specifications. The basic 14-model range was much the same as before, but it now included a 149 cc ohv three-speeder, the model X34-0 at £29 17s 6d, and a good looking 498 cc (63 × 80 mm) ohv V-twin, the J34-11, costing £67 10s and based on a design that had been specially prepared for the War Office. The only other twin was the old faithful 986 cc model, now offered with a hand-change, three-speed box at £72. All the machines were now equipped with electric lights and horn as standard.

In the 24 months since the last show there had been great improvements in general design and in the quality of equipment. There were several 'show surprises', undoubtedly the most prestigious being the centrepiece of the BSA stand — a 500 cc ohv machine with fluid-flywheel transmission and preselector gearchange mechanism. These worked on the same principles as had been developed by the Coventry division for use with Daimler and Lanchester cars, the latter marque having, a year or so earlier, been added to the BSA group of companies.

The fluid flywheel machine was basically a 495 cc ohv, upright, single-cylinder job, the main difference in the engine being the left-side flywheel which formed the driving member of the fluid arrangement. It was considerably wider than the standard wheel and was hollowed out. Inside the hollow was the driven member and both wheels had vaned troughs, almost filled with a special, non-freezing liquid. When the driving wheel revolved it carried the liquid with it; centrifugal force caused the fluid to move outwards and the curved edge of the trough threw it across to the driven member where it impinged on the vanes to impart corresponding rotary motion. The system did not depend at all on viscose drag, but relied solely on the momentum, or kinetic energy, of the fluid. The primary drive from driven member to gearbox was by oil-bath chain, in a 1½:1 reduction ratio. The gear mechanism was contained in a separate case, bolted to the back of the engine. There was no need for an engine-shaft shock absorber or a clutch. In the gearbox was a three-speed epicyclic system, in constant engagement. According to whether the internally toothed annulus, the star-wheel assembly or the sun wheel were locked by band brakes, so were the required gears brought into use. The same principle was employed in Model T Ford cars.

Gear changes were effected by preselecting the ratios by means of a small handlebar lever (with 1, 2, 3 and Neutral positions marked), cable-connected to the box, and by depressing a pedal. The rider set the lever to the desired gear and at the appropriate moment pressed the pedal; the band brakes did the rest. Alternative primary drive sprockets offered two sets of ratios — for solo use, 4.9, 7.45, 12.8:1; for sidecars, 5.8, 8.7, 15:1. The transmission was of the cross-over type, the secondary chain being on the machine's right side and, as there was no mechanical connection between gearbox and crankshaft, the kickstarter was arranged to operate through the timing gears. It was possible to throttle down to a standstill and accelerate away without changing from the top gear setting. Priced at £70 with full lighting equipment, the fluid-flywheel BSA weighed 370 lb.

The 1933 Show was quite successful and reflected improving trading conditions. Early in 1934 BSA reported a motor-cycle sales increase of 66 per cent on the previous 12 months; at 70 per cent, the three-wheelers showed an even better return, the four-cylinder model having enjoyed a particularly warm reception.

Perrigo, Povey and London's racing sidecar exponent Gordon Norchi frequently formed a

BSA tricycle team, and in the 1933 London-Exeter event Perrigo won a silver medal, failing only on the notorious Simms Hill which floored all of the ten trikes in the trial.

Not two months of 1934 had passed when Small Heath introduced a new 250, the model B34-17, a single-port ohv which, with a four-speed gearbox, gave a better performance than the standard job and, at £48 10s, was cheaper than the 250 Blue Star.

Having made a faultless performance in the Easter-tide London-Land's End trial, Bert Perrigo ended his spell with three-wheelers and came back to the classic 'one-day opens' on his 350 Blue Star with a smashing success in the Mitchell trial — the only rider with a clean sheet. In May Harold Flook was the best sidecar driver in the 'Scottish' and, on her 250, Marjorie Cottle took the Ladies prize.

In the autumn J. W. Bryan was appointed to the board of BSA Cycles Ltd. He had been with the company 25 years, having joined as advertising manager in 1909. His directorship was celebrated by the industry at a Show-time dinner at Frascati's Restaurant, where Joe recalled that before joining BSA he had been employed as a printer by Temple Press Ltd, and had been there when the first issues of *Motor Cycling* (1902) and *The Motor* (1903) were published.

Fred Povey and Harold Flook, both using 499 cc machines, were the solo and sidecar champions in the British Experts trial, each repeating previous successes, Flook for the third year running.

So, with the sign of the Piled Arms well in the forefront of both the sporting and commercial sides of the motor-cycle movement, BSA were content to end the first half of the 1930 decade by making only small alterations and additions to their existing models. However, two new de luxe ohv singles were brought out, the R35-3, a 63 × 80 mm, 249 cc machine at £49, and the R35-4, 71 × 88 mm, 349 cc, at £51. With each, the valve gear was similar to that of the ohv twin — push-rods enclosed in a large-diameter tube, inlet side all enclosed, and exhaust springs left exposed for better cooling. The Magdyno, situated behind the cylinder, was driven from a high-camshaft layout and the full dry-sump lubrication system embodied a seat-pillar-mounted oil tank.

Only detail improvements were made to the three-wheelers, still very popular, and the company were doing well with their own sidecars, of which there were six different models.

A notable absentee from the 1935 catalogue was the fluid-flywheel machine. Notwithstanding good press test reports, it had turned out to be a somewhat expensive and very short-lived non-favourite.

BSA front-wheel-drive three-wheeler cars were first made in 1929, with air-cooled, ohv, V-twin 1,021 cc engines. This alternative, four-cylinder, side-valve, water-cooled unit was introduced in 1933, having a transmission system identical with that of the air-cooled type.

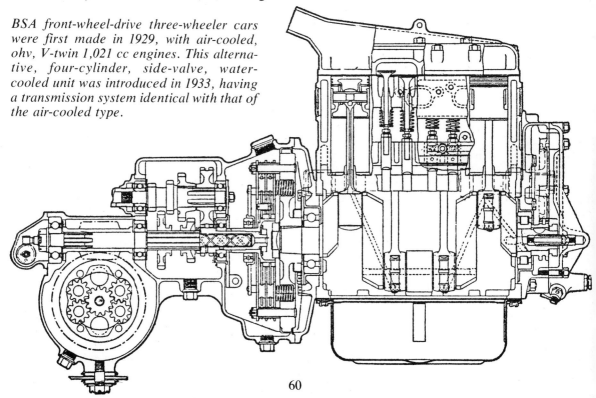

Chapter 11

Star material

'Deliberate speed, majestic instancy . . .' — *The Hound of Heaven by Francis Thompson*

1935 was King George V's Silver Jubilee year. It was also a high peak in BSA motor-cycle history, for it brought the birth of a new breed of models that were to shower honours on Small Heath through three decades. Called the Empire Stars, in loyal recognition of the King's special occasion, these newcomers were not in themselves anything very much out of the ordinary, but they constituted a link with the original red-starred Slopers and Blue Stars. Also, through one machine in particular, as will presently be told, they were directly responsible for a scintillating galaxy of mounts that grew in power, prestige and popularity with each succeeding season.

In actuality, 1935 was a relatively quiet year, so far as BSA Cycles were concerned. Other sections at Small Heath were intensely busy, as Chapter 13 will reveal, but the motor-cycle men concentrated their energies on updating and streamlining an 18-model programme that

catered for practically every rider's needs and pocket. At Olympia, in the autumn, the full range of 1936 products was displayed as below.

The motor cycles, whose prices included electric lights and horn, all had four-speed gearboxes except the 149 cc and the two cheaper 249 cc models. Foot-change levers were standard on the sports types. There were no longer any inclined engines, all the singles having vertical cylinders whose barrels and piston rings were made from an exceptionally tough nickel-chrome iron, calculated to give very much longer life. The use of this special material was BSA's answer to a problem that had afflicted the whole industry around this time — increasingly high piston speeds, coupled with the deleterious effects of the newly arrived leaded petrol, were causing excessive bore wear in barrels cast in the traditional grey iron.

As well as the Empire Stars, there was another

Model	Engine	Exhaust Up/Down	£	s	d
Solos					
X0	149 ohv 1-port	D	31	7	6
B1	249 sv		35	10	0
B2	249 ohv 1-port	D	38	7	6
B18 light de luxe	249 ohv 1-port	D	42	0	0
B3 de luxe	249 ohv 1-port	D	49	17	6
R4 de luxe	348 ohv 1-port	D	52	0	0
R19 de luxe comp model	348 ohv 1-port	U	58	0	0
R17	348 ohv 1-port	D	55	0	0
R20 New Blue Star	348 ohv 2-port	U	58	0	0
R5 Empire Star	348 ohv 2-port	U	62	0	0
W6	499 sv		56	10	0
Q7	496 ohv 2-port	D	59	10	0
Q21 New Blue Star	496 ohv 2-port	U	61	10	0
Q8 Empire Star	496 ohv 2-port	U	65	10	0
J12	498 ohv twin		70	0	0
M10	595 sv		63	10	0
Y13	748 ohv twin		75	0	0
G14	986 sv twin		75	0	0

Sidecars		£	s	d	Three-wheelers	£	s	d
21-44	Special sports	17	0	0	Twin de luxe	98	0	0
21-20	Medium tourer	17	0	0	4-cylinder standard	125	0	0
21-40	Large tourer	20	0	0	4-cylinder de luxe	128	0	0
21-42	Launch	22	10	0				
6B-6	Standard tourer	20	0	0				

newcomer in the shape of a bigger edition of the 500 cc War Office-type V-twin. The latter machine had a pleasantly smooth performance, but was more complicated and really no faster than the ohv singles of equivalent capacity. Also, it lacked the punch needed for hauling anything but a light sidecar. Therefore, it was given an extra quarter litre (71 × 94.5 mm, 748 cc), called the model Y-13 and was put in the catalogue as being especially suitable for third-wheel work, along with, and at the same £75 price as, the everlasting 986 cc side-valver. Also for passenger use was the model M-10 595 cc sv single in a cradle frame which, as with all the other machines, embodied the I-section forged backbone.

Overall responsibility for technical development was then in the hands of David Munro, and to him goes the credit for the two handsome Empire Stars, distinguished by golden, star-shaped emblems on the tanksides embellished with an eye-catching pale green enamel. Mechanically, the most obvious external change was the transference of the Magdyno to a position in front of the cylinder over a large sump. Except that it had a stiffer flywheel assembly and a more highly tuned engine, the 350 cc model was generally similar to its Blue Star companion.

Replacing the abandoned 500 Special, the 500

'An engine which should make a name for itself', was Motor Cycling's *comment on the 1935 496 cc ohv Empire Star unit. It did; with a Brooklands Gold Star (100 mph lap) to its credit, it sired the much-loved, long-lived line of BSA 'Goldies'* (Motor Cycle).

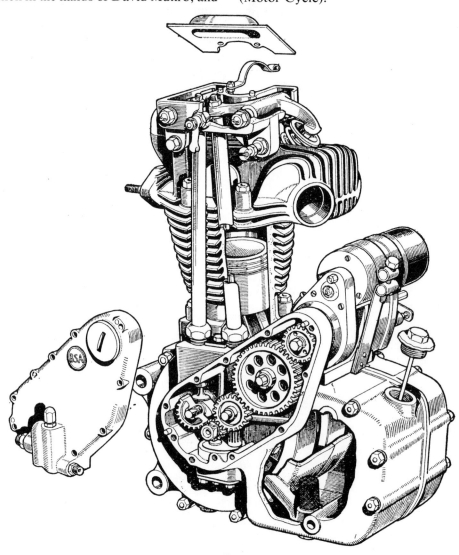

Empire Star was even more highly developed, having a completely new design of cylinder head and other modifications claimed to give a 100 per cent knock-proof performance on a compression ratio lowered from the Blue Star's 6.8 to 6.59:1. Head and barrel were held down by four long bolts passing through the cylinder finning into the crankcase. Bore and stroke were changed to 82 × 94 mm, 496 cc, as against the earlier 499 cc, and all the half-litre ohv singles were so altered after the Empire Stars had been subjected to a great deal of testing and research, on the bench and at Brooklands. The bigger engine peaked at 5,300 rpm and had a power curve that not only climbed higher, but was flatter. On both models, crankcases and gearbox shells were treated with a patent Bakelite lacquer, giving a semi-glossy exterior, proof against heat and oil stains. And they had smooth-surfaced, highly polished aluminium oilbath primary chaincases.

Motor Cycling's drawing of the 500 Empire Star unit was captioned 'An engine which should make a name for itself'. This prophecy it immediately proceeded to substantiate for, in November, it successfully underwent an arduous week's endurance test officially observed by the ACU. The plan was to cover 500 miles at over 70 mph at Brooklands, and then to do a further 1,000 miles on the road, including all sorts of going such as climbs of famous trials hills. The brand-new machine, fully equipped with lights and standard silencers, circled the track at lap speeds of around 77 mph, stopping every half hour for replenishments. The anticipated 70-mph average was actually bettered to 73.3 mph. The subsequent road route involved climbs of the West Country hills Porlock, Lynton and Beggers' Roost; Gloucestershire's Birdlip and Nailsworth Ladder; Wales' Bwlch-y-Groes; and Lakeland's Kirkstone, Whynlatter and Honister Passes. At the end of the 1,000 miles, fuel consumption worked out at between 50 and 55 mpg. The original set of tyres were used throughout and no replacement parts were needed.

After this *tour de force* there was an uncharacteristic lull in BSA competitions activity. The works riders, Perrigo, Jack Amott (returned to replace the departed Povey), Flook and Marjorie Cottle, never got among the premier award winners in the 1936 'opens', and the company did not enter a manufacturers team in the ISDT.

During the year Joe Bryan had taken over the managing directorship of BSA Cycles Ltd, and at the September dealers' convention at Small Heath it was announced that he would introduce the 1937 range. It was well known that at the time he was in South Africa on a business trip. However, the lights went out and there, on a silver screen, appeared J.W.B., in the effective, and then novel, form of a talking picture. What he had to talk about was a 14-model display of machines, all of which, except the 750 and 1,000 cc twins, were singles of entirely new design. Immediately apparent to the delighted dealers was the influence of one of the most gifted engineers the motor-cycle industry has ever known — Valentine Page.

Quiet, thoughtful Val Page had learned his craft in the Tottenham, London, factory of JAP engine makers, J. A. Prestwich Ltd. From there he had gone, via the Triumph company, to Ariel where, in conjunction with another talented Londoner, Edward Turner, he had helped mightily to restore the fortunes of the Selly Oak enterprise when John Y. Sangster, son of founder-director Charles Sangster, took control. 'Mr Jack', as he was always known in motor-cycling circles, combined a clever head for business with a trained mechanical mind, attributes that enabled him to select the right men as his lieutenants and to evaluate the potentialities of a good design when he saw one.

Sangster had, in fact, learned his engineering on the Continent and then in the Rover company's workshops in Coventry. The simple, yet efficient, little air-cooled, flat-twin Rover 8 and the Ariel car which preceded the Austin 7 were two of his contributions to motor transport. With his encouragement, Edward Turner gave the motor-cycle world the unique four-cylinder Square Four Ariel and later the equally famous Triumph Speed Twin design, and Val Page produced a series of singles that were classic examples of the engineer's dictum, 'To be right, it must look right'.

Having done that at Selly Oak, Val had carried his drawing board across Birmingham to Small Heath and there set to work reshaping a full house of machine types that had become bewilderingly diverse. At last, the complex system of model classification was rationalised into just three divisions. The 150 cc machine was dropped and all lightweight 250s and 350s were catalogued in the B group. All the other singles, from 350 to 600 cc, came into the M group and the Twin group still offered the ohv 750 and sv 986 cc V-engined mounts. The Blue Stars and the three-wheelers were discontinued.

For his single-cylinder engines Val Page provided a fully brazed-up frame with one top tube replacing the forged backbone. The ohvs all had single-port heads but twin ports were available on some models if required.

The most outstanding differences on the Page engines were the absence of the crankcase sump, rearward mounting of the Magdyno and an improved method of enclosing the valve gear. This last-named departure was particularly noticeable on the ohvs, which had a separate, tower-like aluminium casting to surround the pushrods; and, for the first time, there was complete coverage for the whole of the overhead gear. The enclosure method for the side valves not only encased the springs and stems but also induced a cooling draught through a passage between the chest and barrel. The larger svs were given two guides per stem, one up and one down. Air-hardening of cylinders was claimed to reduce wear.

Common to all the 1937 singles was a full dry-sump lubrication system incorporating a separate tank and a worm-driven, double-gear pump working in a protruding housing cast at the base of the right-side crankcase half. Where duplex cradle frames were used, the lower right-side member had to be bowed to accommodate the oil-pump housing, a characteristic that persisted for many years, and constantly baffled 'bitsa' builders who tried to put BSA engines into other people's frames.

Apart from the B25 350 Competition model, which had a high-level exhaust pipe secured by a finned nut, and a tubular silencer, the singles had pipes simply pushed into the port and held in position by straps clipped to the frame. Large, parallelogram-shaped, fish-tailed silencers were commendably efficient in a period when the law was more than customarily conscious of 'noisy motor cycles'.

To become long-lived firm favourites, the M20 (500 cc) and M21 (600 cc) side-valve tourers made their first appearance. All the 500s had the high bore/stroke ratio of 82 × 94 mm, 496 cc. The capacity of the 350 types was 348 cc (71 × 88 mm), save for the M19 ohv de luxe which measured 68.8 × 94 mm, 349 cc. The quarter-litre group, which now included a baby brother for the Empire Stars, all had 63 × 80 mm, 249 cc engines.

Pride of the programme was the 500 Empire Star, which had been further developed with a stiffened-up crankcase carrying two main bearings on the drive side. Each engine was given special tuning treatment.

And when the range went on show display it was for the last time at Olympia. The new Exhibition Hall at Earls Court was nearing completion and was almost ready to become the future motor cyclists' mecca.

Customarily a Boxing Day event, the London-Exeter trial had to be postponed to January 1937. In it, Birmingham dealer E. F. Cope caused a stir when, driving a BSA four-cylinder model, he was the only one of a dozen three-wheeler finishers to win a premier award for an impeccable performance. Craftily, Frank Cope (who later turned to road racing, from which he was stopped only when the authorities said he was getting too old) had rigged a Velocette two-stroke engine into the tail of his trike, so that he had a driven rear wheel. He used this adaptation in many events with great success, to the chagrin of the sidecar men, who could find nothing against it in the competition regulations!

With the newly introduced B25 350 Competition model, Bert Perrigo won the Rotherham club's Lister Trophy trial and followed up with best performances in both the Colmore Cup and Victory events. In the latter, the best sidecarist was Midlander Harold Tozer (Ariel), who had already made a racing reputation on three wheels with Norton outfits on the Donnington circuit. Harold Flook had changed to Nortons and BSA had no sidecar driver to take his place.

After tying for premier honours with Yorkshire's Allan Jefferies (Triumph) in the Wye Valley trial, Perrigo announced his retirement from competitions, except for the six-day events. Always on BSAs, he had six times represented Great Britain in the ISDT, had been solo British Expert twice and had made best performances in practically all the British open trials during his ten years with Small Heath. He had been appointed BSA area representative for the West Country.

The situation for a sidecar teamster did not long remain vacant for, at the 'Scottish', Harold Tozer turned up with a BSA outfit instead of the Ariel on which he was entered. He won a silver plaque, and Perrigo was runner-up to winner Jack Williams (Norton), beaten by only one mark.

Having won the International Trophy in Italy the year before, Great Britain staged the 1937 ISDT in Wales, and BSA entered Perrigo, Jack Ashworth and Harold Tozer, all using 496 cc engines, plus Marjorie Cottle with her 250. Bert and Jack won gold medals; Harold crashed on the first day.

And now one of the most — possibly *the* most

— portentious of happenings in the BSA sporting saga occurred, almost casually, on a summer's day at Brooklands. The occasion, on Wednesday, June 30 1937, was an ordinary, unimportant, mid-week handicap meeting organised by the British Motor Cycle Racing Club. In the normal course of events it would have been run off without any special notice, just another of the scores of such matey little get-togethers that the track boys enjoyed amongst themselves. There was, however, something very different about this one, for there in the programme was the entry, W. L. Handley (500 BSA). What made it especially interesting were the facts that (a) Walter Handley had retired from his brilliant racing career two years previously; (b) he had never before been associated with the Small Heath marque; and (c) BSA had not made an entry in a race since their 1921 TT debacle.

Bert Perrigo has recalled how the BSA-Handley combination came about. The competitions department, delighted with the performance of Val Page's new big Empire Star, was toying with the idea of giving it a public — but, cautiously, not too public — airing in a speed event, and somebody persuaded Joe Bryan to sanction a Brooklands tryout. Who should ride it? There was a suggestion that Wal Handley might be willing to de-mothball his leathers, and Perrigo undertook the arm-twisting at the Midland Aero Club, Castle Bromwich, then a rendezvous for a number of motor-cycle folk who had taken up flying. Handley and Velocette's designer-racer Harold Willis shared a venerable Bristol Fighter. Geoff Davison, winner of the 1922 Lightweight TT with a Levis, and at that time my employer, was the owner of a succession of different light aircraft, and Harry Perrey, Perrigo and Povey were keen members.

The deal was made under a cloak of secrecy that in no way deceived the BMCRC handicappers, and when Wal pushed the Empire Star off in a programme-opening, three-lap, outer-circuit race he was in the tail of the field. His helpers were Jack Amott and ex-Humber and Triumph trialsman Len Crisp, who had prepared the machine under the aegis of David Munro, Val Page and his assistant, Herbert Perkins.

For many years 'Bemsee' had conducted the happy practice of awarding little lapel badges to members who lapped the track at 100 mph or more. These awards were no more than shirt-button-sized, yellow-metal emblems, but they weren't easy to acquire and their possession signified entry into an élite coterie of trackmen, the Brooklands Gold Star holders. Wal Handley earned his in that first race, winging the BSA through to finish first at an average speed of 102.27 mph, with one lap at 107.57 mph.

Busy with TT reviews and preliminaries for the ISDT, the motor-cycle press had little space to report the meeting, but there was jubilation at Small Heath, from whence flowed glowing advertisements hailing the 100 mph success. And no time was lost in capitalising on it for, when the 1938 range was revealed in August, it contained an entirely new model directly developed by Page from the track mount. Catalogued as the 500 cc model M24, it was naturally named the Gold Star.

Whereas the Empire Star was an iron-engined job, the new arrival had an aluminium head and barrel with an Austenitic iron liner, the 82×94 mm, 496 cc, configuration being retained. The two-part, polished pushrod tower was cast integrally with head and barrel, sealing of the assembly being made solely by the four long holding-down bolts. Much attention had been paid to weight reduction; high-tensile, light-gauge steel tubing for the frame and Elektron alloy for the gearbox shell helped towards a total weight of only 315 lb, as against the Empire Star's 350 lb.

The 500 Gold Star was listed as a high-speed tourer or as a competitions mount, the main differences being in the tyres and exhaust pipes ('knobblies' and high level pipes for trials work). With full equipment, the touring type was road-tested by *Motor Cycling,* returning a 92 mph maximum on a top gear ratio of 4.8:1. It was also said that there was to be a racing version with a high-compression piston, Amal twin-float carburettor and a top speed of over 100 mph. Prices were set at, tourer, £82 10s; competitions model, £85; and track racer, £92 10s. Actually, very few of the racers were ever built, for these were the days when speedwork was the province of the race-bred marques, such as Norton, Velocette and Excelsior, whose overhead camshaft engines had been developed to a fine pitch of speed and reliability.

One private owner of an M24 who often appeared in the results lists of English and Irish races was Roy Evans. On the other side of the world, where 'Beesas' had many friends, three Australians had regular successes with their Gold Stars — Harry Hinton, Eric McPherson and Tony McAlpine, all of whom were to become renowned in the Isle of Man and on the European circuits.

Chapter 12

Silver, gold and black-out

'They talk of some strict Testing of us . . .' — *The Rubaiyat of Omar Khayyam*

When the new 'Goldies' made their public debut in September 1937 it was in the elegant and spacious setting of the just-completed Earls Court Exhibition Hall, and the Motor Cycle Show was the first of the innumerable attractions and entertainments that have, in 40 years, been staged there. The Earls Court building, with its underfloor pool, convertible galleries, annexes, car parks and Underground station, had taken two years to construct, on a former exhibition site that, with its famous Big Wheel, Flip-Flap and other fairground features, had provided amusement for Londoners since Victorian times.

Many people in the motor-cycle community had mixed feelings about leaving Olympia, particularly regretting the loss of the popular exhibitors' restaurant in the Pillar Hall. Here the catering was in the hands of 'Joe Lyons' (whose headquarters were next door at Cadby Hall), and many important deals were made and contracts fixed over excellent meals swiftly served by smartly uniformed waitresses, the celebrated Nippies of Corner House days. There was no denying, however, that the amenities for the turnstile customers were infinitely better at Earls Court, and the greatly increased floorspace available to the exhibitors encouraged lavish displays and gave much scope for the stand designers.

As the year was ending Perrigo and Tozer were solo and sidecar premier award winners in the Alec Ross trial, which began the winter season's series of open events. Frank Cope got another gold medal in the London-Exeter, with his duo-engined three-wheeler (a performance he repeated in the 'Land's End'). At the dealers' annual convention in November at Small Heath, managing director Bryan said that in the past 12 months 19,000 BSA motor cycles had been sold. Registrations of new motor cycles of all makes had risen from 46,311 in 1935 to 56,077 in 1937.

Early in the new year BSA introduced a 63 × 80 mm, 249 cc sv, three-speed lightweight. Listed as the model C10, it had coil ignition with the skew-gear-driven distributor stuck up out of the timing case; with electric lighting it cost only £37.

February 1938 saw the commencement of another Maudes Trophy marathon that lasted eight days. A list of over 1,000 BSA dealers was handed to the ACU, who picked at random a 500 Empire Star from Sandums of Tottenham, and a 600 M21 from Godfreys of Great Portland Street. The side-valve machine was taken to Small Heath for the fitting of a sidecar and suitable gearing, all under the eyes of official observer E. B. Ware, a former racing man especially successful at Brooklands with Morgan three-wheelers. Then the solo, ridden by road-race expert E. A. Mellors, and the combination, piloted by R. A. Harris with Ware in the chair, foregathered at Wembley Stadium. The Star had had no preliminary running in.

The first part of the schedule called for 20 consecutive climbs of Bwlch-y-Groes, after which the machines went to Brooklands for fast touring, acceleration and brake tests. In six hours running on the track the solo did 127 laps, fastest at 72.71 mph and averaging 58.59 mph. The sidecar outfit covered 100 laps at 46.12 mph with a best circuit at 50.58 mph. Timed over the flying kilometre, their speeds were 78.94 and 56.26 mph respectively.

Then it was back to the Bwlch for another 20 ascents but, on the way back, London had to be crossed from east to west and south to north with gear levers fixed in top. In all, each machine covered some 1,450 miles and the organisation was supervised by David Munro, who did the cross-London sidecar driving, and Jimmy Simpson, the AJS/Norton racer and record-breaker who had become the Shell-BP company's motor-cycle competitions manager. The combined efforts of all concerned gained BSA the Maudes Trophy for the third time.

With Bert Perrigo away in South Africa and Marjorie Cottle now riding Triumphs, BSA were thinly represented in trials, but Jack Amott won the solo Cotswold Cup on a 250 model.

The Gold Star opened its long innings as a scrambles mount when a 350 model, ridden by Lancastrian Cliff Clegg won the first-ever IoM Grand National, held during TT week over a boggy, rocky course inside the race circuit near Windy Corner. A number of the English rough-riding stars had brought their machines to compete and the event attracted such a huge crowd that the Mountain road was blocked from Cregny-Baa to Ramsey.

When the teams were selected for the 1938 ISDT, back again in Wales, there were no BSA riders in either the Trophy or Silver Vase squads, but the company's works trio were Amott, Ashworth and R. E. Spokes. Reg Spokes had won a gold medal the previous year when he was a BSA private owner. Competition for the military team prize, presented by Germany's motor sport leader, General Hühnlein, was keen, for the war departments of the interested nations saw in the ISDT a grand opportunity to test their motorcycle equipment. The ill-omened Hitler/Chamberlain meeting had 'guaranteed' peace in our time, but time was likely to be, as with so many other things, in short supply.

The British Army entered three teams, that of the Royal Tank Corps being an all-BSA one with Sergeant J. T. Dalby and Corporals F. M. Rist and R. Gillam in the saddles. In the club team section the Civil Service Motoring Association had an all-BSA trio and among the private entrants were Harold Tozer and Mrs Miriam Anning, a West of England enthusiast who rode a 249 cc machine. The RTC's chance of winning the Hühnlein prize disappeared on the fourth day when Corporal Gillam had to retire, so breaking up the only British Army team still intact. Corporal Fred Rist finished with a gold medal; Jack Amott sacrificed only one mark and he and Spokes received silver medals; Ashworth got a bronze. The British Trophy team of George Rowley (AJS), Vic Brittain (Norton), Jack Williams (Norton) and Stuart Waycott (Velocette and sidecar) won the trial with a total loss of only nine marks; runners-up were Czechoslovakia with a score of 504. In both cases the only men to lose marks were the sidecar drivers.

A revised group-classification system was adopted for BSA's 16-model 1939 range. The C group contained the 250 cc lightweight machines, namely the C10 in standard and de luxe guise,

One of BSA's most successful lightweight fourstrokes was the 248 cc Model C11, launched in 1938, with crossed pushrods in an integral tunnel, coil ignition and a separate dynamo (Motor Cycle).

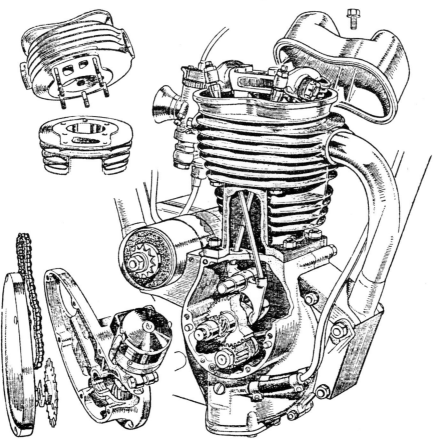

and the C11, a new ohv having a single camshaft with cranked cam followers operating crossed pushrods after the manner of an earlier Francis-Barnett design. A dish-shaped cover, held by one bolt, enclosed the rockers. All three machines had coil ignition and the C10, still costing £37 in standard form, was given dynamo lighting. The 250 cc Empire and Gold Star types were gone.

In the next group came the B models, leading off with the B21 standard and de luxe 250 ohvs and the B23 350 sv, also in two versions. Three new 350 ohv machines were the B24 Silver Star, B25 competition model and the B26 tourer.

In the Medium class came the M20 500 sv, M21 600 sv, M22 500 ohv tourer, M23 500 Silver Star and M24 500 Gold Star. Finally, there was the old stager, the G14 1,000 cc big twin. The two Silver Stars were really updated editions of the equivalent Empire Stars, which had been discontinued, and they were distinguished by chrome-plated tanks having silver-sheen panels. Both they and the Gold Stars acquired screwed-on metal star emblems instead of tankside transfers.

All the machines, from the de luxe B21 upwards, except the standard 350 sv, the 500 ohv tourer and the twin, had a new arrangement of the timing gear. The cam pinions ran on fixed posts pressed into the crankcase wall and supported at their outer ends by an accurately machined steel plate bolted directly on to the timing chest, independently of the cover which, although in no way responsible for alignment of the timing mechanism, provided an outrigger bearing for the mainshaft to resist flexing under load. The cam profiles were reshaped for quieter running and the crankcase was further stiffened, with the distance between the two driveside main bearings increased to 1¼ inches for greater rigidity. The cylinder head and overhead valve gear were left unaltered.

The only Gold Star model, the M24 costing £77 10s, had been given detailed improvements, the most obvious being seen on the pushrod tower which had two vertical bolts at the head/barrel joint. Also, the exhaust pipe had a finned nut and the gearbox had exchanged its Elektron case for an aluminium casting containing, for the first time, close ratios of 4.8, 5.1, 8.5 and 11.8:1.

At the end of 1938 Val Page went back to the Triumph company which, under the governance of Jack Sangster, had been reformed as the Triumph Engineering Co Ltd, shedding its affili-ations with cars and bicycles. Page, having given Ariels their fine range of Red Hunters, and BSA their Gold Stars, rejoined, as chief engineer, two former Ariel colleagues, Edward Turner, now appointed Triumph's managing director, and Herbert Hopwood, Val's erstwhile assistant at Selly Oak, who had become chief draughtsman at Coventry. Norton's 'wizard of waft', Joe Craig, was expected to become technical director at BSA Cycles, but the announcement was premature and instead he moved to Woolwich to join the AMC organisation.

A recruit to the Small Heath trials crew, F. C. Perks, made best sidecar performance in the Colmore and Victory events, and in the Cotswold Cups trial the RTC's soldier-riders Corporals Doyle and Rist and Private J. L. Wood, all BSA-mounted, won the team prize against opposition from five other factories. The up-and-coming Doyle also took the best 350 cc award, heading trade experts Len Heath (Ariel), George Rowley (AJS) and Jack Williams (Norton).

Small Heath's success in the Maudes Trophy had revived interest in this contest and, almost at the same time, BSA, Triumph and P & M began ACU-observed tests aimed at capturing the award in 1939.

The BSA effort was again a complicated one. Two machines, a 500 cc Silver Star and an M21 600 cc sidecar outfit, were picked from dealers' stocks, and the scheme was:

1) to ride, without stopping engines, round the England-Wales coastline, approximately 2,500 miles and including 25 climbs of Bwlch-y-Groes;
2) to make a one-hour run across a major town with gearboxes sealed in top;
3) to complete 100 miles of high-speed work at Brooklands;
4) to make 100 ascents of the Brooklands Test Hill.

In charge of the operation were David Munro and W. S. Banner. Formerly a Levis executive and latterly a leading figure in the ACU Midlands Centre, Stan Banner was a member of the BSA sales staff and it was he who, legend has it, persuaded Joe Bryan to allow Wal Handley's historic gold star Brooklands outing. To work in relays, the riders were W. Johnson, W. Goulding, G. Carter, R. A. Harris, Jack Amott and Harold Tozer, with Bert Perrigo in reserve. Roy Evans relieved Amott at half-distance, Jack having a commitment to ride in the Wye Valley trial. Passenger-observers were E. B. Ware, Ken Bilbe and W. J. Bishop.

The start was at the ACU headquarters at 83 Pall Mall, London, on Tuesday March 14 and, when the convoy reached Brooklands on the following Saturday, they were 64 miles short of the stipulated 2,500. This was made up by a trip to Chichester and back. During the 100-mile stretch from Brighton, via Hammersmith and Kingston, to the track, top gear only was used, the levers having been removed.

Roy Evans rode the Silver Star for the 100-mile high-speed track test and averaged 73.68 mph. With the M21 outfit Tozer averaged 48.43 mph.

The Brooklands Test Hill had a mean incline of 1 in 5 over 151 yards, with a maximum gradient of 1 in 4. It had been intended to make 100 ascents in 100 minutes and both machines, which used second gear, bettered the target by over ten minutes.

Because of a fouled sparking plug and choked jets, neither machine actually completed the road course without stopping engines, but when stripped for official examination they were found to be in excellent condition.

Just as in 1914, the splendid summer weather of 1939 was, figuratively speaking, overcast by the clouds of impending war, and what to do about the International Six Days Trial, celebrating its 21st birthday, became a problem. Having won in 1938, Great Britain had the right to host the event, but the ACU had declined and Germany had taken on the organisation, electing, however, not to hold the trial in their own homeland, but in their lately over-run territory of Austria, with the music-centre city of Salzburg as the headquarters. Despite repeated assurances from Berlin that there was nothing to fear, British competitors were reluctant to commit themselves until it was learned that the War Office would be entering three Army teams for the Hühnlein Trophy, with a regular colonel commanding a considerable staff.

Trepidations thus partly allayed, a large British contingent set off in mid-August, not much liking the intense military activity they encountered as they reached the area of France's Maginot Line. And the scene was even grimmer when they found the Germans hard at work on their Siegfried Line, and an acute shortage of petrol along the route to Salzburg.

There were no BSAs in either the Trophy or Vase teams. The works' team comprised Jack Amott (496 cc) Jack Ashworth (249 cc) and Harold Tozer (496 cc sidecar). The Army teams were, respectively, Matchless, Norton and BSA

mounted, the last named having Sergeant Rist, Corporal Doyle and Private Wood as riders. Again the CSMA entered a BSA trio, F. C. Perks, C. Ridgeway and F. P. Whitehouse.

The situation at Salzburg was at first untroubled, except that the British were somewhat put out to find that, instead of the customary road or track circuit for the final speed test, the Germans had chosen terrain closely resembling a scrambles course. However, the organisation was generally efficient, the scenery beautiful and the weather good. The officials, elaborately uniformed in field grey with side arms, jackboots and swastikas, were at pains to brush away any undertones of international tension. Nevertheless, when Lieutenant-Colonel C. V. Bennett appeared in his trim, be-ribboned, Sandhurst-cut khaki, with walnut-hued Sam Brown and glistening cavalry boots, and armed only with a swagger stick, he drew glances in which admiration was probably tinged, especially among the older Nazis, with disquieting memories.

Then, mid-way through the week, came the dramatic change. Germany and Russia had just signed a mutual non-aggression pact. The Germans saw this as a safeguard against strife, but the British took the opposite view, and on the Thursday night the ACU withdrew its teams from the contest. Others were left to decide for themselves whether they would continue, and Colonel Bennett was put in a quandry for he had had no recall instructions from Whitehall. These did arrive later, but by then most of the British party were on their way home, some, me included, to don uniform 'for the duration'.

When the Great Retreat took place, Britain's Trophy and Vase B men, as well as the BSA Army and works' teams, were all unpenalised and comfortably poised to fight it out with the Germans and Italians in the speed test. The trial ran through to the finish, Germany annexing both the Trophy and the Silver Vase, but the governing body, the Fédération Internationale des Clubs Motocyclistes, promptly declared all results null and void. The Trophy itself was ultimately recovered by the Allied Occupation Commission and returned to the FICM for competition when the time was ripe — which did not happen until 1947.

In the dismal, blacked-out November of 1939 the ACU announced the winners of the Maudes Trophy. BSA's coastline/Brooklands test had been in vain — the prize went to Triumph, but nobody bothered very much. There was a far more urgent contest to be decided.

Chapter 13

Articles of war

'Once more into the breach . . .' — *Henry V*

In the near 40 years that have passed since the lights went out over Europe on September 3 1939, Second World War stories have flowed ceaselessly from printing presses, cinema screens and radio and television studios. Great men's memoirs, official archives and documentary researches have told and retold the tales of victories and defeats, patriots and quislings, masterly strategy and bungling muddles so exhaustively that one might think there was no facet of the global struggle left unexplored or unexplained. Yet there still persists a myth that when the Allies and the Axis joined battle, John Bull was caught with his trousers down.

Well remembered are the warnings thundered so ominously by Winston Churchill, but with the passage of the years there seems to have arisen a belief that his was a lone voice crying in a wilderness of couldn't care less. Neville Chamberlain's Munich meeting with Adolf Hitler had bought 'peace in our time', so that when, 12 months later, Britons found themselves at war, they had a feeling the umpire had called 'play' while they were still in the changing room. So runs the latter-day legend.

Of course, it wasn't like that at all. Great Britain was in a far better state of preparedness in 1939 than it had been in 1914, and one story alone, that of BSA, throws a revealing light on how much had been done among the Services and their suppliers to make ready for the menace looming over the Continent.

The stupendous part played by BSA in providing the tools to finish the job has been recorded in a book, *The Other Battle,* produced by the company in 1946 and written by Donovan M. Ward. Sub-titled *A history of the Birmingham Small Arms Co Ltd, with special reference to the war achievements of BSA Guns Ltd and BSA Cycles Ltd, and the other subsidiary companies directly administered from the head office of the parent company at Small Heath, Birmingham,* it takes the reader behind the scenes in the build-up of a vast armaments organisation. It recounts tales of astonishing engineering ingenuity and virtuosity, massive production capacities, incredible blitz resistance and recovery faculties, feats of great heroism among the workers, and

provides scores of instances of the special, long-inherited skills that Birmingham folk bring to the manipulation of metal. Understandably, the book is mainly devoted to the war-time Battle of Production, but perhaps the most surprising revelation among all the facts, figures and statistics, is the extent of BSA's *pre-war* involvement.

After the 1918 Armistice the company had declared their intention, as recalled in Chapter 6, of converting the whole of their plant to the manufacture of motor cycles and cycles 'on a hitherto unprecedented scale'. And to most people, particularly those in the transport industry, it seemed that that was exactly what happened. One was aware, of course, that somewhere in the Small Heath complex there was a BSA Guns division, turning out relatively small quantities of high-quality sporting guns and target and air rifles. But what we didn't know about was BSA's conviction that they had a duty to the nation as well as to their shareholders. Purely out of this sense of responsibility, a large amount of military rifle-making machinery was retained in working order, even though its capital cost and maintenance was an annual debit item on the balance sheet. Any suggestion that it should be disposed of merely brought a reminder from the chairman of the company's title, and that there were things that stood above profit and loss accounts.

For some 17 years these idle machines did not produce a single rifle until, in 1935, there came a contract for 16,000 Lee Enfields for the Iraqui Government. And in that same year BSA started to prepare for the Second World War.

Hitler had been in supreme control of Germany less than 12 months but, as Donovan Ward put it, 'already the sparks of revenge were being fanned throughout the Fatherland — revenge for 1918, revenge for Versailles, revenge for the loss of colonies; above all, revenge on Britain'.

A formidable demonstration of the growing strength of National Socialism was staged at the great Leipzig Fair in 1935. Ostensibly a trade forum, it was also a para-military exercise and the thousands of foreign visitors who attended were treated to displays by marching storm-troopers and given many other evidences of

Germany's war-like ambitions.

Among the visitors were two executives from the Birmingham Small Arms Company, the senior being James Leek who, when we first met him in Chapter 8, was driving a sidecar outfit in a BSA works trial. On his return to Small Heath, Leek presented his report to the directors. 'We are going to be forced into war,' it stated, 'and we must have a substantial sum to bring the organisation up to date and to fulfil our obligations to the country'. Despite the difficult times that had been experienced since 1918, and without any financial backing from the Government, which at that time was pledged to international disarmament, the board courageously sanctioned the heavy expenditure called for by Leek's report and the factory, quietly, without relinquishing its normal occupations, resumed its familiar mantle as a private arms manufactory.

Thus it was that, when war was declared, BSA's planning office and toolroom had been on overtime for three years; a seven-day week with overtime had been worked for months in those sections of the plant already making armaments; in some shops a night shift had been operating for a year. Work at Small Heath, apart from secret weapon research, included the manufacture of Browning machine guns, Boys anti-tank rifles and magazines, Lee Enfield Mk III rifles, Bren gun parts, fuses, primers, 40 mm shells, and gun carriages. A new Redditch works was turning out 7.92 and 15 mm Besa machine guns.

James Leek became managing director of BSA Guns Ltd and was the mainspring behind these intense years of pre-war activity, just as he was the key man throughout the war when the whole of the BSA organisation grew into an enormous empire spread right across the country. Between 1937 and 1945 BSA made 468,098 Browning guns for the Allied air forces, sufficient to equip 60,000 eight-gun fighters. Production was running at close on 17,000 guns a month in 1942 and a similar output of Hispano Suiza 20 mm cannon was reached in the summer of 1943. Oerlikon cannon, Bofors AA guns, naval pom-poms (the celebrated 'Chicago pianos'), rifles, sub-machine guns, pistols and rocket projectiles streamed in staggering quantities from BSA's own plants, from the works of other companies taken over by the Small Heath administration and from BSA-supervised sub-contracting firms. Under Small Heath control were 67 establishments, employing 28,000 workers and 25,000 machine tools. More than 5,000,000,000 munitions components were made by BSA Guns and BSA Cycles for the battle against the Axis — an average of 1,650 pieces every minute, day and night, from the first 'Take cover' to the final 'All clear'.

Along with weapon making went a spiderweb of allied activities, such as research and design for special products, like rotor blades for jet engines; chemical and metallurgical work, in which the BSA-owned, Redditch-based company, Monochrome Ltd, led the world in highly advanced metal-treatment techniques; and an intricate inspectorate organisation, at its peak engaging a staff of 2,500 men and women who, in liaison with the Government's own officers, 'viewed' some 2,000,000 precision components every day, the average BSA output through the six years of fighting.

And what about BSA's wheeled vehicles? For example, the most successful fighting vehicles in their class used by the Allies were the BSA Scout light reconnaissance cars and their later, heavier versions, the Daimler Mk I armoured cars. Both were evolved in the Small Heath design department, so thoroughly that in the six years of their use in all theatres of operation not a single major modification to the original concepts had to be introduced.

Plans for the Scout were laid down in 1938 when the War Office was seeking a counterpart to the German army's gun-carrying, semi-armoured motor-cycle combinations. In collaboration with the Wheeled Vehicles Experimental Department at Farnborough, the BSA team produced a prototype whose main features were four-wheel drive from a central differential, fluid-flywheel transmission from a 2½-litre Daimler engine, independent suspension, a speed of 60 mph forward and 55 mph in reverse, with steering at both ends. Being only 5 ft high, it presented a minimal target area and the angling of the seven-millimetre armour plating gave the two occupants of the turret protection equal to plating of double the thickness. The prototype car passed its tests, including a 10,000 mile road trial, with flying colours and in January 1939 came an initial order for 500 Scouts. But where to build them was a problem. BSA's Birmingham plants were already overstressed, particularly with Browning gun production, and the shadow factory at Redditch was still being completed. The answer was the Daimler factory at Coventry, from whence the engines would come anyway, and where Daimler designers were working on the larger Mk I model.

At that time no one envisaged a desert war, but it turned out that both the Scout and the Mk I might almost have been specially designed for the soft-sand conditions of the North Africa campaign. Indeed, Rommel chose a captured Scout in which to make his escape after Montgomery's defeat of the Afrika Korps at El Alamein.

*   *   *

To recall the two-wheeler contribution made by BSA Cycles Ltd there can be no better way than to reproduce in full the two chapters which *The Other Battle* devotes to these aspects of the Small Heath war effort. Under the heading *Army Motor Cycles,* Donovan Ward wrote:

The men who had made BSA the greatest motor-cycle manufacturers in the country were not switched to gun production on the outbreak of war; a great many were needed to produce the vast numbers of machines required by the army.

The close collaboration on design and production which had existed between the War Office and the company in the Great War had been revived in 1932 when BSA was asked to evolve a special 500 cc twin-cylinder model, a type then favoured by the military experts because of its great flexibility. So successful was the resulting machine that not only were substantial numbers supplied to the army, but a large order was also placed by the Air Ministry.

Personnel changes at the War Office in 1937 led to an alteration of policy, the new regime favouring a 500 cc single-cylinder side-valve engine. Both BSA and the Norton Company submitted modified versions of their standard models of this type to the Mechanization Experimental Department at Farnborough for tests, which included a 10,000 mile reliability trial in very exacting conditions.

At this period the European situation was so forbidding that army officials began to make plans to provide the thousands of motor cycles which would be needed immediately if it came to war. The hampering hand of the Treasury, even then not reconciled to spending money on rearmament, was seen in their first proposal — that BSA should permanently keep in stock large numbers of machines, which the Government would buy if the necessity arose. Despite the fact that it involved locking up considerable capital in goods which could not be sold on the civilian market, the directors took the view that, if this were the only way in which the needed reserves could be created, the company should agree to it in the national interests. But before they could give formal assent to the scheme, it was abandoned by the Government in favour of direct purchase.

Simultaneously with the putting forward of this plan, a complete list was compiled, largely through the help of BSA, of all stock in dealers' hands throughout the country, stock which could be impressed in emergency.

While these preliminary defence schemes were being considered, the company did not lose sight of the fact that its products must be made even more popular in the Service than they already were and teams of Army riders, mounted on BSA motor cycles and coached by one of the Small Heath experts [Bert Perrigo] competed in all the leading trials. Their outstanding success came in 1938 when, on 500 cc single-cylinder overhead valve Gold Star models, they were awarded in the International Six Day Trials in Wales the trophy for the best performance by a unit of the British Army. Whether by coincidence or whether this influenced the War Office is not known, but the fact remains that a few days later a large order was received at Small Heath for the 500 cc side-valve machines, which had been under test at Farnborough [Militarised M 20 models].

During the spring and summer of 1939, the company made elaborate preparations to capture some of the chief trophies at the International Six Day Trials to be held in Germany in August. On the penultimate day, however, instructions were received from the British Ambassador in Berlin for the teams to withdraw at once and return home owing to the imminence of hostilities.

In the 12 months before the war BSA supplied more than 3,000 motor cycles to the army, not only the 500 cc models but also 250 cc lightweights, which had first been ordered for training purposes in 1937.

On the outbreak of war the Government requisitioned every suitable motor cycle the company had in stock — 690 machines — and in addition placed an immediate order for 8,000.

It was not only Britain who wanted motor cycles: South Africa, Eire, India, Sweden and Holland were clamouring for them. The biggest overseas orders came from the Dutch Government, which had switched from German makes to BSA the previous year, and in view of the fact that Holland was a potential ally the company was allowed to fulfil them despite our own shortage at the time. Altogether in the two years before the occupation of the Netherlands by the Nazis, the company supplied the Dutch Army with more than 1,750 motor cycles of the 1,000 cc and 600 cc types.

On the collapse of France, BSA set out to help to make good the colossal losses of equipment, which included every motor cycle that had been taken by our expeditionary force to the Continent. The need was desperate in view of the invasion menace, and output was increased from a steady 500 a week until it attained a figure of 1,000 a week, at which rate a finished machine was coming off the production line every five minutes.

During those first hectic months of the war BSA delivered the prototype of a special light 350 cc motor cycle, which the War Office had asked the company to design for easy handling in bad road conditions. The Service experts were highly delighted with the trials and an order for 10,000 was received within a few days of their completion. It was, however, never executed. Before the necessary planning could be carried out, the order was altered to the 500 cc models already in production. The reason for the change was that there would be complications in spares and maintenance if the army had two main BSA types in service.

Not only was the company interested in supplying motor cycles to the army; it was also deeply concerned that the best service should be obtained from them. To make this possible it was suggested to the War Office that some of the company's experts should give tuition both to the men who would be riding the machines and also to those who would be responsible for their maintenance, especially in the abnormal conditions of desert warfare. The offer was immediately accepted and, in the course of the war, lectures and practical demonstrations were given to more than 250,000 officers and men in all parts of the country. Over the whole course of the war period output from the company's works totalled 126,334 of the 425,000 motor cycles supplied to the War Office by British manufacturers.

Thus did BSA Cycles sustain their slogan, 'One in four was a BSA'. And this was the tale of the *Paratroop Folding Bicycles:*

Every bicycle used in action by British parachute or airborne forces during the war was manufactured by BSA, to the original designs of its technicians. The landings in North Africa in 1942, the D-day invasion of France, the glorious tragedy of Arnhem, the first employment of Allied paratroops beyond the Rhine when the Sixth British and 17th American airborne divisions were dropped between Xantend and Wesel in front of Montgomery's advancing forces — at all these milestones on the road to final victory these bicycles were used.

As soon as war started, BSA received orders for the standard Mk V military bicycles, but they were not needed in the numbers used in the Great War. The day of the long forced march into battle had passed; the day of the mechanised infantry who followed closely behind the tanks in motor transport had come. But in the very advance of the science of warfare a new use was created for the bicycle — it would be ideal for paratroops if a suitable type could be evolved.

In 1941 the company was asked by the War Office to design a folding bicycle, which could be strapped to the back of a paratrooper. It was obvious that the BSA folding bicycle of the Great War, the first of its kind to be invented, would be useless however much modified; it was altogether too heavy.

The specification called for a machine of not more than 30 pounds. Using standard parts and normal design, the company's technicians, at their first attempt, produced a bicycle weighing 32 pounds. This was overweight, but at their next effort they evolved another model which only just turned the scale at 28 pounds. On submitting it to the War Office, however, they were informed that the specification had now been altered and that the machine must not weigh more than 25 pounds. Before they could even start work on this, the War Office again made a change and stipulated a machine weighing not more than 22 pounds.

This was obviously impossible to achieve with normal design; something completely unorthodox would have to be found. Before the war one of the BSA cycle experts had been considering an alteration in the standard type of frame, which had remained virtually unchanged throughout the industry for 42 years. Setting to work on this new principle, a folding cycle was evolved which weighed only just on 21 pounds.

The War Office experts, while delighted with the machine, were at first doubtful as to whether it would stand up to the work for which it would be needed. It did not appear to them robust enough to be ridden over rough country. But the confidence of the BSA men was justified for in its official tests it withstood infinitely harder usage than any paratroop operation could involve. So impressed, indeed, were the American and Soviet military representatives, who were present at the demonstration, that the prototypes were immediately sent to the United States and to Russia.

In these trials, incidentally, the bicycles were not strapped to the backs of the paratroopers since it had been found that if, on landing, a man fell backwards heavily, he was liable both to injure himself and his machine. Instead the bicycles were tied to parachutes in batches of three and dropped at the same time as the men, who picked them up on landing.

Here it may be mentioned that the War Office made it clear in the beginning that the effective life of these bicycles need only be 50 miles but, in fact, they did more than 500 miles in the official tests without showing any signs of wear, while many of them, used for ordinary purposes, exceeded 10,000 miles.

In June 1942 the War Office placed contracts for 15,000, demanding the first deliveries within five weeks. The prototypes had been made in the toolroom and the order involved making all the necessary fixtures and jigs. Before the month was up, however, output had started and from 100 a week it rocketed until in the seventh week 1,000 were produced.

The insistence of the War Office on early deliveries could be understood in the light of later events, for this was the time when final preparations were being made for the British-American landings in North Africa.

Altogether more than 60,000 folding paratroop cycles were manufactured by the company, a figure which equalled the number of ordinary military cycles it delivered during the whole course of the war.

Although not introduced as having any specific connection with vehicles, there is another story in *The Other Battle* which does, in fact, have a direct link with motor cycles.

In December 1938, only ten days after Chamberlain's return from Munich, there arrived at Small Heath Frantisek Janacek, son of Dr F. Janacek, a Czechoslovak arms manufacturer.

The visitor was accompanied by one of the Prague company's technical staff, an Englishman who performed the introductions and acted as interpreter. They explained that they had no faith in Hitler's promises and were convinced that in a few months Germany would seize Czechoslovakia. The Janaceks had been working on a new type of gun and ammunition for their own army, and they wanted their potential allies, Britain and France, to have the benefit of the project. Prototypes were already in being, but Frantisek Janacek wished to continue his research free from any possible German interference.

To the BSA technicians the Czech design appeared to have valuable possibilities and the upshot was that Janacek began work at Small Heath. His English companion returned to Prague. Although not named by Donovan Ward, he was, in fact, G. W. Patchett, a much-experienced Brooklands man and a clever engineer. Like several other British motor-cycle experts, notably Walter Moore, who had gone from Nortons to NSU in Germany, and Dougal Marchant, a Chater-Lea exponent who had joined Motosacoche in Switzerland, George Patchett had in the mid-1930s moved to the Continent to become technical director of Janacek's Jawa motor-cycle division. There he designed and developed racing machines and lightweight two-strokes that performed with distinction in international competitions, including the TT and the ISDT, always with George himself in charge of his enthusiastic teams.

Patchett had hardly got back to Prague when his fears were realised. In March 1939 — only four months after research on the Janacek gun had begun at Small Heath — the Germans marched into Czechoslovakia and within hours Nazi experts, primed by spies, were searching the Jawa factory for the secret weapon. But all traces of it had disappeared. Acting on a tip-off, Patchett had, the night before, delivered the prototypes and the relevant drawings to the British Legation for onward transmission to the War Office. Defying all the conventions of diplomatic immunity, the Germans subjected the departing British officials' luggage to intensive searches, but the Foreign Office knew a thing or two and, three months later, the cases containing the guns were in London awaiting collection by BSA personnel.

And George Patchett was also back in England, reunited with Frantisek Janacek in pursuing the research work at Small Heath. In May 1939 they both visited my Birmingham office and we went together to *Motor Cycling's* Donington Day race meeting. So convincingly emphatic were they that it was only a matter of weeks before Britain would be at war that, despite my resolve to go to Salzburg for the ISDT, I went out and joined the Auxiliary Air Force.

George went back to Prague to rescue his family and was again involved in a cloak-and-dagger adventure. Hidden in his car were the latest blueprints of the secret gun, and when he reached the German frontier into France he found the guards and Gestapo men 'on parade,' listening to a Hitler broadcast. They were so busy 'Heil Hitlering' that they paid scant attention to the travellers and the Patchett party, and the drawings, went on their way unhindered. On September 6 1939 a *Motor Cycling* writer remarked: 'Those of you who have been enquiring anxiously after George Patchett and family will be relieved to know that they are safe and well. We had a post-card the other day from a holiday resort in France'. Later George, as did many other motor-cycling technicians, moved into the 'back room' world of Britain's armaments boffins.

After some lengthy tests the Janacek project failed to gain War Office approval, but Small Heath persevered, eventually obtaining a Whitehall grant in aid and finally triumphing when more tests revealed such a remarkable ability to pierce armour plating at long range that the gun was hailed as the answer to Germany's Tiger tanks. Production was fully under way by mid-1942 and design details were passed to the USA so that, when D-Day came, the Littlejohn guns and projectiles, as they had become known, were used with great effect by the British and Americans against the German self-propelled guns.

Frantisek Janacek's father had not been able to prevent the Nazis from obtaining details of the weapon which, in a modified form, was used against the Russians in 1942. But it had to be abandoned because the Germans were unable to obtain supplies of tungsten carbide, a material essential to the gun's effectiveness. On the other hand, the British Government decided that its performance was so good that it warranted the setting up of special factories to process tungsten brought from the Far East.

The weapons research laboratories which Frantisek Janacek had joined had been set up in 1935 by F. W. Hulse, who had relinquished the position of works manager to devote his whole energies to the study and development of rocket missiles. Another of the company's engineers of the 'old school,' James Dickinson, became works director and held that vital post right through the war until 1954.

The potentialities of rocketry, especially in a war context, had received much attention on the Continent since the late 1920s, a leader in the field being car manufacturer Fritz von Opel, who had built successful rocket-propelled vehicles and boats. Even so, it was Britain who first used rockets in the Second World War, and much of the credit for this goes to Freddie Hulse, whose knowledge of the subject had become so valuable that, in 1936, BSA lent him to the Government. He joined the scientists who, led by Sir Alwyne Crowe, Director of Ballistic Research, were already working at Woolwich Arsenal in an experimental department that was to become the Projectile Development Establishment. Mr Hulse not only evolved special fuses and projectors but acted in liaison with BSA who were, from 1937, making the prototypes of projectiles which passed their tests in the spring of 1940. Production was in full swing at Small Heath when, in November, an air raid necessitated removal of the work to a dispersal factory at Tunstall, near Stafford. The machines were restarted there in January 1941 and thenceforward the demand for projectiles became so great that the company's works at Coventry, Tyseley, Redditch and Small Heath were all contributing to the main output from Tunstall.

During the course of the Luftwaffe's blitzkrieg, BSA factories were many times hit and temporarily immobilised, and none suffered more heavily than Small Heath. The company founders' acumen in siting their first factory at a junction of the Grand Union canal and the London-Birmingham main railway line had the disastrous consequence of providing the German navigators with a readily recognisable prime target, and on the night of November 19 1940, a few days after the notorious Coventry raid, the whole area was subjected to a vicious attack that almost completely demolished the New Building, which was making Browning guns, Fifty-three employees, nine of them women, were killed and 89 injured, 30 seriously. For their heroism under air attack many of the workers received awards, two of them George Medals. For their parts in keeping the plants going at this and at other periods of the war, four of the company's staff were named in Honours Lists. James Leek was made a Companion of the Order of the British Empire, Bill Rawson and Albert Wood became Members of the same Order, while F. T. Whitehouse was awarded the British Empire Medal.

Chapter 14

The Roaring Forties

'All things bright and beautiful' — *Mrs Alexander*

The blackout came down and the lights went up — and up with them went the motor-cycle movement into an epoch of activity that seemed almost unbelievable to those who had experienced the creeping paralysis of the Thirties. From a record high of 731,298 motor cycles running on British roads in 1929, the annual registrations had declined steadily to 278,300 ten years later. Yet within 12 months of the end of World War Two there were 462,327 machines in use and over the next 12 years the graph surged upward like the contours of the Matterhorn. The 1929 record was passed (over 750,000 machines) in 1950, the million mark was hit in 1953 and in 1958 the peak was reached at over a million and a half.

But that was only one side of the picture. Along with home sales went a huge output for an avid world-wide market. Indeed, for several years after the war the tag 'for export only' was applied to the latest models and British riders had to wait until production attained sufficiently high levels to provide for both overseas and domestic demands.

First rumblings of the approaching boom came from the English factories early in 1945. In that year, on January 4, a BSA advertisement announced: 'While Jack Service [symbolising all serving men] is putting the finishing touches to Jerry, we at BSA are adding the finishing touches to that long-awaited post-war BSA motor cycle.'

Victory was in sight, and the motor-cycle makers were already preparing to switch tank finishes from khaki to chrome. Those firms, particularly BSA, Matchless, Norton and Triumph, which had supplied the bulk of military machines, were naturally in the best position to make a quick change, and the race to be first with a peace-time programme was actually won by Triumph, who paraded a range of Speed Twins and Tiger models in March. Associated Motor Cycles followed quickly and in August Small Heath opened their stall for civilian customers.

By this time Sir Bernard Docker, son of Midlands industrialist Dudley Docker, had succeeded Sir Geoffrey Burton as chairman of the Birmingham Small Arms Company. James Leek was its general works manager and a director of BSA Cycles and BSA Guns, of which James Dickinson was works manager; John E. Rowe was financial director, Bill Rawson was service manager, George Savage home sales manager; Noel Brealey, for many years Joe Bryan's advertising and publicity lieutenant, had taken over the department; Bert Perrigo was supervising the experimental and competitions aspects, Bert Hopwood, David Munro and Herbert Perkins plied their slide rules and T-squares in the technical design and drawing offices. Stan Banner

This company 'tree' shows the structure of the BSA group as it was in 1946. Small Heath Administration was directly responsible for the management of all the companies stemming from it.

The Birmingham Small Arms Company Ltd

| The Daimler Co Ltd
Lanchester Motor Co Ltd
Transport Vehicles (Daimler) Ltd
Birtley Co Ltd
Hooper & Co (Coachbuilders) Ltd
Barker & Co (Coachbuilders) Ltd | William Jessop & Sons Ltd
J. J. Saville & Co Ltd
Bromley, Fisher & Turton Ltd | Small Heath
Administration | BSA Tools Ltd
Burton, Griffiths & Co Ltd
BG Machinery Ltd
BSA Grinding Machine Co Ltd
BSA Automatic Machine Co Ltd
Arthur Andrews Ltd |

| BSA
Guns Ltd | BSA
Cars Ltd | BSA
Cycles Ltd | BSA
Radio Ltd | Monochrome Ltd
of Redditch | Cycle and General
Finance Corporation Ltd |

| Sunbeam
Cycles Ltd | New Hudson Ltd | The New Rapid
Cycle Co Ltd | Ixion Cycles Ltd | Eadie
Manufacturing Co Ltd |

had rejoined his former company, Levis Ltd, as general manager.

The widespread ramifications of the Birmingham Small Arms Company, as they were at the war's end, are shown in the table on page 76, reproduced from *The Other Battle*. The bicycle companies constituting the lowest branch of the 'tree' included the renowned Sunbeam name, which had been acquired from Associated Motor Cycles during the war. Not shown was another important addition, made in December 1944, when Jack Sangster, managing director of Ariel Motors Ltd, sold the share capital of that concern to BSA. The transfer caused a sit-down strike among the people at Selly Oak, but when they learned that the Ariel marque was to continue in its old home they went back to work.

Four models composed the first post-war BSA range. Three of them were essentially 1939 types, the 250 cc C10 sv and C11 ohv, and, shorn of its army accoutrements, the 500 cc M20 sv. Altogether new, to civilians, was a mount that was to become a hardy annual in Small Heath catalogues and is still a much sought after model among collectors and restorers, among whom is no less an enthusiastic owner than the publisher of this book, Mr Patrick Stephens!

The B31, as the new arrival was designated, required no preparation to get it on the market for it was, in effect, the special Silver Star-based 350 cc machine that had been evolved for the army but which, as mentioned in Chapter 13, had been rejected by the War Office after successfully passing its official tests. The only obvious difference between the 'civvy' model and the prototype, apart from a black and chrome finish instead of camouflage, lay in the overhead valve layout — double coil-springs were fitted instead of hairpin springs. An M20-type bottom half, using the Val Page timing-gear arrangement, carried an iron barrel (71 × 88 mm, 348 cc), topped with an iron head on which was a fully enclosing alloy rocker box; a separate polished aluminium pushrod tower had a removable cover plate at the base to allow access to the adjustable tappet heads. With ratios of 5.6, 7.3, 11.1 and 15.9 to 1, the compact, foot-operated gearbox included drive for the tank-mounted speedometer.

Without doubt, the most striking feature of the new B31 was its telescopic front fork. Oil-damped 'teles' had been pioneered on German BMWs in the late 1930s, and during the war AMC had introduced their celebrated Tele-draulics for army Matchless machines. The B31 pattern, patented by Herbert Perkins, was so neat and efficient that it not only became a standard BSA component for many years but was also frequently substituted for their original forks by owners of other makes of machine.

M20 models were ready for delivery as soon as they were announced; the others became available in September and October, and there was only one snag. The basic prices compared favourably with pre-war figures, but for home buyers these had now to carry Purchase Tax. An indication of what this impost meant is seen in the following table:

Model	Retail price			Purchase Tax			Price with Tax		
	£	s	d	£	s	d	£	s	d
C10 250 cc sv	63	0	0	16	3	5	79	3	5
C11 250 cc ohv	66	0	0	16	18	10	82	18	10
B31 350 cc ohv	86	0	0	22	1	6	108	1	6
M20 500 cc sv	96	0	0	24	12	10	120	12	10

Unless otherwise ordered all machines were fitted with speedometers, adding £4 8s including Purchase Tax.

Small Heath had loudly proclaimed that this quartet was only the beginning of a much wider range which the backroom boys were preparing, and before 1945 was over it was known that a BSA vertical twin was on its way, and it was an open secret that something very special would soon be appearing with the highly revered Sunbeam name on its tanksides.

The eagerness of the factory men to get back to conditions under which they could exercise their ingenuity and expertise, unhindered by the dictates of military necessities, was equally matched by the enthusiasm of the prospective customers, impatient to lay their hands on the twistgrips of new, exciting, personally owned machinery. Even at this early stage, the organisers of sporting events were broadcasting their plans for the resumption of the classic competitions. Despite petrol coupons, the ACU was issuing permits for old favourites like the Colmore and Victory trials; the Isle of Man was promising a Manx Grand Prix in 1946; and in Ireland scrambling and road racing had already restarted.

No one was surprised, therefore, when, in January 1946, BSA came out with a competitions edition of the B31. With a high-ground-clearance frame, wide-ratio gearbox, upswept exhaust pipe and lots of chrome on mudguards, stays, rims, brake plates, etc, the B32 looked, and was, at a basic £100, a winner.

The Sunbeam rumours turned to fact when, in March 1946, a remarkable 500 cc ohc parallel-twin cylinder machine, combining car and motor-cycle design practice, was introduced to the technical press. Listed as the Sunbeam Model S7, it was the work of Erling Poppe, member of a family famous for their achievements in internal combustion engineering. Coventry-built White and Poppe engines powered pioneer motor cycles and were the first units to be used in Morris cars. In the mid-1920s the P & P motor cycle was outstanding for its novel design; the initials stood for Packman and Poppe. As one of James Leek's team of technicians, Erling Poppe included among his war-effort contributions the development of the Scout reconnaissance car, and in producing the S7 he was working to a brief from Leek who, appreciating the high-quality standards that had made the John Marston Sunbeams' reputation, directed that: 'Our aim must be a motor cycle as modern as tomorrow, but built in the famous tradition — a judicious blend of originality and the orthodox. Within these limits the designer can start with a clean sheet of paper and really let himself go.'

The result was a machine that had its car-like engine-clutch-four-speed-gearbox unit disposed longitudinaly in a duplex cradle frame, with shaft drive to an underslung worm and wheel assembly enclosed in a massive alloy case. The heavily ribbed alloy crankcase-cum-cylinder block was a fine piece of foundry craftsmanship. The cylinders (70 × 63.5 mm, 497 cc) had steel liners and the Y-alloy head enclosed valves at 22 deg operated by rockers from a chain-driven camshaft on the rear end of which was the ignition distributor. The pancake-type dynamo was attached to the forward end of the crankshaft. Both exhaust ports and the inlet tract were on the right side of the head.

A salient feature of the S7 was the attention paid to rider comfort and convenience. A pivoted, soft-top saddle was adjustable for rake and load, had a wick-lubricated spring working inside the top tube and there were additional Silentbloc supporting members. The 4.75 × 16-in balloon tyres were specially moulded by Dunlop for the extra-wide rims and the mudguards were proportionately generous. Plunger-pattern rear springing was of normal design but the front fork was unusual in that the stanchions acted solely as telescopic struts, the suspension member being a separate unit between the legs. Shock and recoil springs took all the loading, there being no fric-tion or hydraulic damping effect. Despite this, the big tyres and a dead weight of 390 lb, the machine steered perfectly, smoothing rough roads in a manner never before experienced by the pressmen who tested the prototype. The price, without tax, was £175.

Two additional versions were proposed; one a rigid-framed job and the other a Sports edition, having a different cylinder head with 90 deg valves in hemispherical combustion chambers and a crossflow inlet and exhaust system. It was capable of 95 mph, but neither it nor the rigid model ever reached the market. Some two years later the Model S8, with a rather more utilitarian specification, joined the S7, and many thousands of both types were made before they were discontinued in 1958. The Redditch-built Sunbeams were never intended for competitions work, but, with an S7 outfit, one-legged sidecar expert Harold Taylor won a gold medal in the 1949 ISDT.

Just before the war, visitors to Armoury Road might have glimpsed BSA testers going about their duties on prototypes of a model that was to have been the next Show surprise. Close examination would have revealed a vertical-twin engine that bore a strong resemblance to a much earlier unit of that type — Val Page's 650 cc Triumph Model 6/1, which first appeared in 1933 and preceded the Edward Turner Speed Twins by five years. Except that it was a 500 and had fully enclosed overhead valve gear (rocker boxes integral with the head), the BSA twin repeated most of the characteristics of the Triumph 6/1, including a single, behind the cylinders, camshaft operating tappets and pushrods located in a tunnel through the block casting. Page was actually back with Ariel by 1939, but there was such a close likeness between his first twin and the BSA job that it seems likely he had laid the plans for the latter type before his departure.

At all events, the war stopped production and no more was heard of the newcomer until March 1945, when its engine layout was described in a patent specification taken out in the name of BSA, claimed advantages being that a single camshaft saved man-hours and material costs. Eighteen months later, in September 1946, the complete machine was on sale as the Model A7, worthy sire of a long-lived line of powerful, reliable parallel twins that carried the Piled Arms trademark.

The Model A7 had engine dimensions of 62 × 82 mm, 495 cc, and, like the Triumph 6/1, was of semi-unit construction, that is, the self-contained gearbox was bolted to the back of the crankcase, with duplex-chain primary drive. Respectively fore and aft of the cylinder block were the chain-driven dynamo and the geared magneto. The rigid, duplex cradle frame had a telescopic fork, the total weight was 365 lb, top speed 90 mph, basic price £135. A rear-sprung model was promised for the near future.

In the spring of 1947 came the expected 500 cc version of the very popular B31; with measurements of 85 × 88 mm, 499 cc, the B33 was otherwise almost identical with the smaller machine. A competitions edition, the B34 soon followed and the pre-war 591 cc sv M21 and the 499 cc M33 ohv reappeared, both, like the M20, having girder forks. The C11 250 cc ohv was provided with a de luxe blue and chrome trim and alternative finishes were optional on the other models. The 'winged B' BSA motif, adopted in 1946, figured on the tanksides of all ten of the models composing the range for 1948, and there was a sidecar with an attractive semi-sports touring body.

*   *   *

'Designed and constructed to the requirements of a special overseas contract, a new BSA light-weight two-stroke unit has been announced'. So ran the March 1948 press release heralding one of the best-loved, most completely successful motor cycles ever produced by BSA — perhaps even by any company.

The brief specification accompanying this 'export only' announcement was:

52 × 58 mm, 123 cc; 180 deg transfer ports; plug entering at cylinder rear; flat-top piston; four long bolts holding head and barrel to crankcase; alloy head; iron barrel; single-lever, ⅝ inch bore Amal carburettor; Wico-Pacey lighting and magneto-generator; in-unit three-speed, constant-mesh gear set with concentric foot control and kickstarter; intermediate ratios 2.24, 3.76 and 7.05:1; unit weight 45.5 lb.

'Whether we shall eventually see it housed in a BSA frame,' wrote *Motor Cycling*, 'is a thought to be considered — time may show!'

Time did show, and quickly. In June came the first appearance of the Model D1, having the stroker unit mounted in a rigid frame with a non-hydraulic tele fork. Quantity production began a month later at the Redditch factory, in company with the Sunbeams, and the Bantam, as it was now called, was launched, at a basic £60, on its distinguished career. It was finished in a pleasant shade of pale green, a colour that had

also replaced the initial, traditional, black and gold on the Sunbeams.

At the first post-war Earls Court Show of 1948 the BSA stand displayed a 14-model range, among the major attractions being the new Bantam; a de luxe plunger rear-sprung A7 called the Star Twin; and a return to the fold of the Gold Star name, linked with a brace of B32 350s, one for competitions and one for scrambles. Very much in the 1939 style, the motors, designated ZB types, had alloy heads and barrels, with the pushrods passing through an integral tunnel to rocker boxes cast in with the head. Designed for 'pool' petrol, these engines produced 24 bhp at 6,500 rpm and, in plunger-sprung frames, were immediately successful.

The enormous potentialities of the North American market were now being exploited by the British motor-cycle industry, and in February 1949 the whole of the BSA range was exhibited by the company's East Coast US distributors, the Rich Child Cycle Co, at the New York Show.

At home, S. F. Digby, general manager of BSA, Sunbeam and New Hudson Cycles, was appointed to the board of BSA Cycles Ltd. Stan Digby had joined in 1945 as general sales manager of the parent company. R. J. 'Bob' Fearon, who had spent all his working life with BSA and who had been one of James Leek's chief assistants on Browning gun production, transferred to Triumph as works director. Bert Hopwood, after launching the A7 model, had gone to Norton, there producing the renowned Dominator Twin that became the basic design of that company's motor cycles through the next 20 years.

As the decade drew to a close the BSA programme had grown to 17 individual models, most of them variable by alternative specifications. Telescopic forks were standard equipment. Plunger rear-springing figured only on the Gold Stars and the Star Twin but the others, including the Bantam but excluding the M types, could be so fitted at extra cost. The Bantam had a competitions variant, there was an 85 × 88 mm, 499 cc, B34 Gold Star and, with a four-gallon tank, the pride of the package was the new A10 Golden Flash, a 70 × 84 mm, 646 cc big brother to the A7.

With a galaxy of famous stars stacking up successes in trials, scrambles and racing, and with an insatiable demand from all over the world for mounts that suited every type of user, BSA's motor-cycle men rode into the 1950s with a boom like a sonic bang.

Chapter 15

Stars in their courses

'The world's great age begins anew, The golden years return . . .' —*P. B. Shelley*

VE Day, May 8 1945, had seen the end of Hitler's Reich. Japan's capitulation was still to come, but within a couple of weeks of Germany's surrender the British Government had launched the basic petrol rationing scheme.

From June 1 all motorists and motor cyclists could obtain coupons allowing them to buy limited amounts of commercial-grade 'pool' petrol, freed at last from the 'essential war work' stipulations that for six years had proscribed the private use of motor vehicles.

The basic ration for motor cycles was meagre enough — two gallons a month for machines under 250 cc and three gallons for bigger mounts. But it was sufficient to set long-idle wheels rolling again, and almost at once the motor-cycling journals began to carry reports of sporting competitions run for civilians, instead of having to tantalise enthusiasts with accounts of strictly military events, as they had been doing through the final phases of the war.

The immediate post-war contests had of necessity to be planned to meet rationing. Long-distance races were out; short circuits were in. Trialsmen adopted the 'pocket-handkerchief' course, compressing a maximum of hazards into a minimum mileage.

Very early on the scene of sport revival were the Irish. In June 1945 the Ulster MCC staged a 'grand reunion' grass-track meeting at Dunmurry where pre-war stars like A. J. 'Artie' Bell, Ernest Lyons, Terry Hill and the McCandless brothers, Rex and Cromie, found themselves beset by a tough, hard-riding young Ulsterman from Bangor Castle, William Nicholson. Finishing third to Lyons and Bell, on a well-worn, home-tuned 350 Beesa, Bill Nicholson made the debut that was to lead to his ten-year reign as a BSA superman.

A month later, the Ards MCC ran the first post-war road race over a circuit around Nicholson's home town, Bangor, Co Down, and Bill, now in the Experts class, brought his 350 into second place between the 500s of Ernie Lyons and Rex McCandless. Lyons's mount was a sprung-rear-hub Triumph Speed Twin; Rex was aboard the Triumph-engined Special of his own devising, with a unique duplex-tube frame and

pivot rear springing system that eventually developed into the renowned Norton 'Featherbed' layout.

Throughout the summer, trials, scrambles and sprints were held all over the UK and in November came the restoration of the big, trade-supported open trials, beginning with the Gloucestershire-based Stroud Team trial with 35 teams and an almost equal mixture of old and new hands among the 190 individual entrants. Carrying off the team prize were the BSA trio of Bert Perrigo, Jack Amott and Jack Blackwell, riding 350s that were actually prototypes of the competitions version of the B31, announced in the following January as the B32.

Opening the 1946 series of big-time trials, the Colmore Cup saw the principal awards going to the pre-war experts. Demobbed and now on the Small Heath competitions staff, ex-Sergeant Fred Rist was the winner and Fred Perks (496 BSA) was the best sidecar performer. Second-best soloist was Bill Nicholson, who was in an all-Irish BSA team with Artie Bell and Terry Hill. Nick's performance won him instant membership of Perrigo's works squad and the Ulsterman soon afterwards began his lengthy career in the experimental shop in Armoury Road. Fred Rist followed up his Colmore success with a best solo ride in the Victory trial and, with Blackwell and Nicholson, took the one-make team prize for BSA. In the Cotswold Cups event old-timers Harold Tozer, Fred Rist and Fred Povey were all cup winners.

And so it went on, with Rist, Nicholson and Tozer appearing in the headlines week after week — and Small Heath were pressed to meet the demand for B32s.

Isle of Man racing was resumed in September 1946 when the Manxmen succeeded in accumulating enough petrol to run a splendid reunion Manx Grand Prix. But only one enthusiast, Harry Boynton, ventured to enter a BSA, and that failed to finish the course. At that time the competitions department in Armoury Road had little interest in road racing; trials were their forte, extending to scrambles as their men particularly Nicholson, began to notch up victories over the rough stuff. Harold Tozer, using

44: *With new, CB-type Gold Stars, BSA riders made a near-clean sweep of the 1954 Senior Clubman's TT. The winner, Alastair King (No 46) shakes hands with runner-up Ben Denton; between them, in cap, is ex-MGP star, Denis Parkinson, president of the BSA Owners Club.*

45: *With an alloy cylinder head, the 500 cc Shooting Star was a high-performance variation on the iron-engined A7 vertical twin. First produced in 1954, specially for the American market, it remained in BSA catalogues until the end of 1962.*

46: *Ace moto-crossman Geoff Ward, for many years an AJS rider, had a spell aboard BSAs. On this occasion, February 1956, he was testing the possibilities of a proposed scrambles course in Lord Montagu's Beaulieu Park, Hampshire.*

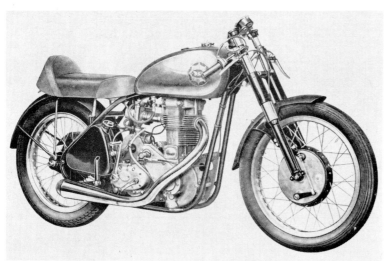

47: *(Left) With a BB-type 500 cc engine in a rigid frame, and with many other fit-for-the-purpose features, this was how BSA specially prepared their Gold Stars for the 1954 Daytona Beach race.*

48: *(Below left) Gold Stars, set up in business-like trials trim, won innumerable premier awards in the days when big four-strokes dominated competitions. This is how they looked around 1953/54.*

49: *(Below) For a time, around 1955, Clubman's Gold Stars were available with both CB- and DB-type engines. This big-fin job had the latest engine but retained the standard handlebar brackets, abandoned in the following season.*

50: (Above) An intermission of 35 years separated these two 250 cc mounts — the 1924 side-valve 'Round-tank' and the 1959 ohv C15 Star, straddled by BSA's then newly appointed competitions manager, Brian Martin.

51: (Right) Star Twins — the A50 (499 cc) and A65 (654 cc) — appeared in 1962, with engine-gear unit construction, die-cast light alloy cylinder heads and 12-volt electrical equipment. In this picture of three good-looking models, the motor cycle was the A65 version.

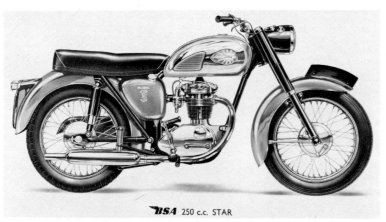

BSA 250 c.c. STAR

52: *Introduced in 1958, the ohv, unit-construction 250 cc C15 Star was one of BSA's most successful designs, both as a roadster and a sports mount, becoming a platform from which many larger versions were launched.*

53: *Competitions editions of the 250 Star model were marketed early in the 1959 season, with both trials and scrambles specifications. This was the C15T Trials Special.*

54: *Clearly a derivative of the C15 250 Star was the 343 cc Model B40, a 1960 Show surprise replacing that long-lived favourite, the B31.*

55 & 56: *The unit-construction, vertical-twin layout introduced in 1962 was used by BSA to power a number of basically similar models with equipment selected to suit specific markets, at home and abroad. For example, the standard Star Model A65 (above), with valanced mudguards and enclosed rear chain, was offered as a de luxe roadster, while the Rocket A65R (below), with a high-compression engine, slim guards, siamesed exhaust system and a generally sportive specification, was essentially a roadburner.*

BSA 175 c.c. Bantam Super model D7

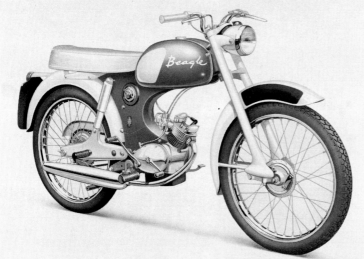

57: *(Left) Becoming more and more sophisticated, BSA's two-stroke model, having grown from 125 to 150 cc capacity, reached 175 cc in 1958 when, with hydraulic suspension fore and aft, it was listed as the D5 Bantam Super.*

58: *(Below left) A 75 cc ohv engine in an open, pressed-steel, swing-fork frame, and a front fork with leading links, were features of Edward Turner's 1962 creation, the Beagle Model K1. A somewhat similar 50 cc companion was called the Ariel Pixie.*

59: *(Bottom left) A Beagle frame with a front down member, a 125 cc Bantam engine, a Bantam fork and an Ariel Leader silencer figured in this circa-1963 experiment which never reached the market.*

60: *(Above right) Like the Beagle-Bantam, the 1962 Rocket Gold Star was a hybrid, combining a high-performance A10-type engine with a frame and gearbox of Gold Star origin. The front fork and exhaust system came from the Rocket A65R.*

61: *(Right) BSA's first and only International Tourist Trophy was won in the Sidecar Race of 1962, when Chris Vincent, passengered by Eric Bliss, averaged 83.57 mph with his own 'home-built' outfit, powered by a much 'breathed-on' 497 cc Shooting Star twin engine. Then employed in the Armoury Road test shop, Chris still turns out with his BSA specials.*

62: *With an engine strongly reminiscent of a 250 C15 Star, the 441 cc Victor Grand Prix, first made in 1964, was a formidable contender 'over the rough' before light two-strokes came to the top in international moto-cross.*

63: *As was its 1961 predecessor, the Sport Star 80, the SS90 was developed from the 343 cc B40 model. With a 90 mph maximum, it was one of the fastest roadster 'three-fifties' to come from Small Heath.*

his long-toothed but extremely reliable 496 cc outfit, was the 1946 British Sidecar Expert. Nicholson (B32) was runner-up to Bob Ray (497 Ariel), the Solo champion.

These were the days when trialsmen mostly pinned their faith to hefty 'singles' tuned to produce tremendous torque 'low down' and to 'plonk' like gas engines at next-to-no revs. Anything below 350 cc was regarded as a tiddler, fit only for boys and beginners. BSA needed a half-litre mount to challenge the Ariels, Matchlesses and Nortons, and when it came, early in 1947 in the shape of the 499 cc B34, Nicholson, Rist and Co really got going. Bill and Harold pulled off a double in the Victory trial, although Harold was still using, as he did for many seasons, his favourite 496 cc engine. They repeated the performance in the Alan and West of England events and Bill won the Reliance trial, in which Harold was not competing. In the British Experts, Tozer, and his regular passenger, Jack Wilkes, won the sidecar award for the second year running and Nicholson conceded only one mark to the solo winner, Artie Ratcliffe (Matchless). In the list of finishers was a name that was to rank among the highest in the halls of motorcycling fame — G. E. Duke. Not long released from the Royal Corps of Signals, in which he had been a member of the Motor Cycle Display Team, Geoff Duke first hit the headlines when he won the Cheshire Championship trial on a B32 in October 1947. A first-class performance in the Yorkshire Solo Championship followed and talent-scout Perrigo quickly had the lad from St Helens signed up and working in the Small Heath 'comp shop'.

During the summer of 1947, not with any great show of enthusiasm, and perhaps even with some reluctance, BSA had found themselves once again involved in road racing — and TT racing at that! The previous year's Manx Grand Prix had demonstrated that Island racing had lost none of its appeal, but neither the British nor foreign manufacturers had had much time or opportunity to resume race development work, and it was feared that entries for the International events might be insufficient in themselves to furnish the traditional spectacle. Furthermore, there weren't many racing factories left in the game; in 1939 only two English marques, AJS and Velocette, had made works entries in the TT.

What could be done to recapture the interest of firms whose one-time rivalry had given the races that spice of variety which aroused strong parti-

san support among the fans?

A Clubman's TT was the ACU's solution — Mountain Course races for as-per-catalogue sports models, ridden by club-entered 'non-works' competitors. Very few deviations from standard specifications were permitted; lighting sets could be discarded; straight-through exhaust pipes were allowed, but not megaphones; kick-starters were essential and had to be used, even after pit stops.

The entries — 64 in all — for the 1947 Clubman's races, three capacity classes run concurrently on the Wednesday of TT week, were satisfactory, both in quantity and diversity of machinery. There were four BSAs in the 350 cc Junior class, Fron Purslow finishing fifth and Peter Moss seventh. At half-distance, local lad J. W. Moore had been lying second to the Norton winner, Denis Parkinson, when 'engine trouble' overtook him. H. R. Holding was sidelined by a spill. In the Senior race only two of the 23 starters were on BSAs, a pair of A7 twins. One, ridden by Eric Stevens, was in fourth position on the second lap when a cracked carburettor stopped further progress. N. Kirby's petrol tank split and he managed only one lap. Of the BSA contingent — 'team-managed' by Bill Nicholson — only Moore and Holding had any previous Mountain Course experience, both having ridden in the 1946 MGP.

As was expected, overhead camshaft Nortons — race-bred International models — figured prominently in the Senior event but the winning machine, ridden by newcomer Eric Briggs, was closely chased home by the Triumph of Yorkshire's evergreen veteran, Allan Jefferies.

At the end of the season James Leek gave a party for the BSA/Ariel trialsmen, those present including, under Small Heath colours, Bill Nicholson, Harold Tozer, Fred Rist, Phil Hewitt, Jack Amott, Cliff Holden, Geoff Duke and Bert Perrigo; Selly Oak's men were Harold Taylor, Bob Ray and Jack Stocker.

In the New Year, Duke left for the Norton camp and Hewitt retired from trials, leaving Nicholson, Rist and Tozer to fly the flag while Perrigo, who had given up regular competition riding, looked around for new arrows to restock his quiver.

Using a 'trialised' A7 twin, with which he was never quite happy, Nicholson won a number of minor class awards in the opening trials of 1948 but, back again on a 'single', a new 499 cc B34, he was the only rider not to lose marks in the Victory trial, and during the year he won two other English opens, three class cups and took the Hurst Cup in his native Ulster. Harold Tozer's record in 1948 was again formidable. With the exception of the Colmore trial, in which he had machine trouble, he gained an award in every event he contested, the bag amounting to nine premiers, or opposite class awards, and three class cups.

In the Isle of Man it was a different story. After what had been a not unpromising beginning in the first Clubman's TT, the BSA result in 1948 was dismal. In the Junior race, against a field strong with AJS and Velocette mounts, four of the five BSAs retired and the fifth finished 21st, and last! In the Senior there were only two BSAs and both were early retirements.

After such a cataclysmic debacle it would have been reasonable to prophesy the end of Piled Arms participation in the Clubman's events. But look what happened! In 1949 there were no fewer than 24 BSAs in the Junior race (Norton 14, AJS 10 and Velocette 6). As well as winning the race, Small Heath claimed fourth berth and 14 other placings among the 57 finishers. Only five BSA riders retired and among them was one who had been lying second when a broken chain stopped him on the last lap. The winner, Harold Clark, knocked 50 seconds of the previous year's lap record, raising it to 75.81 mph.

It was a sensational debut for the re-introduced 350 Gold Star, the first of eight successive Junior victories and the prelude to BSA dominance of the Clubman's TT that was ultimately to prove impregnable.

It is now over 20 years since the last Clubman's TT was run, and the tale of the ten-year life of the series could make a book in itself. Regrettably, from the point of view of those who never followed the races, or who cannot now remember all the involved changes of regulations, courses, classes and methods of running the event, no such book has ever been written.

All that chiefly remains in memories is the belief that it was the overwhelming superiority of the BSA marque that finally killed the Clubman's. This is not altogether true, for there were other significant factors that eventually contributed to the ACU's decision to call a halt. For example, long before the end of the run, the original concept — to augment the IoM June programme — had lost its purpose, for not only was support for the International races continually increasing, but the advent of extra events, the 125 cc Lightweight and the Sidecar races, had made it necessary to hold the club classes either before or after the traditional Race Week — an arrangement that was not popular with the competitors or the Islanders.

A comprehensive, blow-by-blow account of BSA's impact on the Clubman's TT would heavily overtax the compass of this work. Nevertheless, due credit must be given to an extraordinary story of success, and readers who can take their facts cut and dried will find a condensed record of Small Heath's achievements set out in Appendix A.

The 1949 Clubman's TT was not the first race meeting at which the revived Gold Star had appeared. James Leek's visit to the New York Show had so impressed him with the enormous possibilities of the transatlantic market that, on his return to Small Heath, he gave instructions for a suitably prepared pair of Goldies to be sent to the States for Americans Tommy McDermott and Gene Thiessen to ride in the commercially prestigious 200-miles Daytona Beach championship, held in March. Against strong competition from ohc Nortons and Harley-Davidson twins, McDermott finished in sixth place.

And, as the decade was closing, Bill Nicholson convincingly 'proved' the 500 Goldie by winning the Yorkshire-based Scott Trial — his third victory in four years of BSA riding in that notoriously exacting classic.

Chapter 16

Ta-ra-ra boom decade (Part 1)

Hos successus alit (Success nourished them) — *Virgil*

News of an important non-event signalled the motor-cycling movement's entry into the second half of the twentieth century. There would, said a new year announcement by the Manufacturers' Union, be no Earls Court Show in 1950 — 'the only justification for a show is found where new designs are to be introduced, or a fillip to sales is deemed desirable. These conditions do not at present exist. Few, if any, radically new designs are likely to be announced within the next 12 months and the need for maximum production of current designs is considered to be essential to the national interests'.

The conditions certainly were remarkable. The total number of motor vehicles on UK roads exceeded four million — an all-time record and over a million more than there had been ten years earlier. When the Second World War ended only 124,000 motor cycles and 787,000 cars were in use but since VE-Day the totals had gone up to 616,000 motor cycles and 2,107,000 cars, despite tremendous problems in re-equipping and re-tooling factories, obtaining materials and satisfying a voracious export market.

Reporting a Ministry of Supply cut in the home sales car quota — a curtailment that meant almost four years wait for a new vehicle — *Motor Cycling* commented: 'it is obvious that the domestic demand for motor cycles and sidecars will increase enormously and this means . . . that our industry has a huge task and wonderful opportunities before it. Never in the history of motor cycling has the potential of newcomers to our ranks been greater!'

The opportunities were taken and the task was performed, with such enterprise and vigour that the 'Fantastic Fifties' will ever be remembered as the golden years for riders of British-built motor cycles.

In upholding their 'leaders of the industry' claim, BSA's part in this brilliant decade was so packed with innovations, developments and successes, both in sales and sports, that its retelling as a continuous narrative could become a mind-boggling exercise. Instead, as was done in *Norton Story,* the most significant happenings and highspots in the 1950-60 period are pinpointed for ready reference in the following 'annual reports'.

1950

Small Heath geared all resources to the job in hand and during 1950 concentrated on output rather than specification changes. The Golden Flash was given a new look with a four-gallon tank, and the 125 cc Bantam was offered in competitions form, and with plunger rear springing.

Personnel-wise, designer Bert Hopwood had returned from Bracebridge Street to Armoury Road. Into the trials team, to support Rist, Nicholson and Tozer, came westcountryman Johnny Draper who, though short of stature, was long on skill and courage both as a 'balancer' and a scrambler; another scrambling ace, former Matchless exponent, the beefy Basil Hall from Dunstable, also joined the squad.

Draper soon made his mark by winning the Irish Hurst Cup trial, beating, on a 350, Bill Nicholson (500) on his native heath. With Rist, they took the team prize. In August Draper demonstrated his all-round ability (a year later he was a placeman in the Clubman's TT) by winning a fiercely fought Moto-cross des Nations contest in Sweden, just ahead of Basil Hall, both riding 500 Gold Stars. Also appearing among the awards lists was a mid-season recruit to the scrambles team, John Avery, from Oxford who, though he could handle a 500 with the best, persistently wiped up the Lightweight races with a 250. However, in the Experts Grand National Nicholson took the lightweight prize on a Bantam.

Bantams were also distinguishing themselves on race circuits and one of the most successful users was J. A. Hogan, a pioneer among the many who have specialised — and still do — in tuning these little two-strokes to produce astonishing results from what was essentially a simple, utilitarian design originated by DKW.

Having seen their chief rivals, Norton and Triumph, do so well in the 1949 Daytona races, BSA made an even greater effort to equip their American riders with competitive machinery and, furthermore, two factory representatives, Bert Perrigo and Cyril Haliburn, were sent to 'the Beach' to give aid to the Gold Star entrants. This time Tommy McDermott finished third in the Experts 200-mile race and another Goldie was fourth in the Amateur 100-miler.

In a Wales-based ISDT, Fred Rist captained a splendidly victorious British Trophy team that did not lose a single mark. Nicholson gained another Scott Trial success, with Draper as runner-up, and they repeated their 1-2 in the British Experts event.

It was in 1950 that the ACU introduced the Trials Drivers Star competition, with solo and sidecar categories and run on a league system of points scoring covering 26 major events. At the season's end P. H. 'Jim' Alves (Triumph) was the winner; Draper, having contested eight trials, was third and Nicholson, with only five rides, was 11th. Harold Tozer swept aside all opposition in the sidecar class, with a score almost double that of the second man.

1951

Search the pages of the contemporary motor-cycling magazines and you will find no mention of what was perhaps the most portentous event in the whole story of BSA. It happened in March 1951, but not until long after did the general public learn that two of the industry's leading companies had amalgamated — BSA had bought up their biggest rival, the Triumph company!

When, in 1944, Jack Sangster sold Ariel to Small Heath, it was agreed that should he ever wish to dispose of his Triumph Engineering Company, the first refusal would go to BSA. Now 'Mr Jack' decided that the time had come to make the offer, which BSA accepted, paying nearly £2½ million for the Coventry concern, which had cost its owner some £50,000 in 1935 and was currently a very wealthy undertaking. Jack Sangster became a BSA parent board director, but the two organisations continued to run entirely separately, and on such a level of intense rivalry that few ordinary folk realised there was any connection between them.

Meantime, the tenour of normal progress under the Sign of the Piled Arms moved on, outwardly undisturbed by big-business dealings in banks and boardrooms.

Additions to the already formidable competitions strength were David Tye, a Derbyshire-man from Matlock, and a red-headed, genial giant from Yorkshire, Tom Ellis. Having a pretty free hand in the Armoury Road experimental shop, Bill Nicholson had developed an almost Meccano-like system for assembling machines to suit the expected conditions of the events to be contested, and one of his main interests at this time was in rear suspension. In his freelance

days he had worked with the McCandless brothers and, having won many trials and scrambles on his own BSA equipped with McCandless springing, he was naturally strongly in favour of the pivoted-fork arrangement. But as a works rider he was committed to use the company's plunger method. Nevertheless, for his personal mounts, he substituted oil-damped units of his own making for the standard plunger internals. With these, plus some covert mods to the teles, he got things just as he wanted them and romped through the 1951 season to top the Trials Star contest with 90 out of a possible 100 points, his victories including the toughest of the lot, his favourite Scott Trial in which he made best performance on both time and observation. In the Experts Trial Bill tied for the solo premier award with the year's most amazing 'discovery', Lancashire-born, Birmingham-raised, 17-year-old J. V. 'Jeff' Smith (Norton).

A Scrambles Drivers Star had been instituted for 1951, covering 12 events. BSA riders took fourth to ninth of the 10 leading places, their order being Draper, Tye, Hall, P. A. Nex, Avery and G. C. Dawson. Phil Nex, a Hampshireman, immediately became a regular BSA scrambler. Basil Hall's placing was particularly praiseworthy because a couple of accidents had kept him out of all but two of the events.

At the Daytona races, 500 cc British machines, mainly Nortons and Triumphs, completely eclipsed the native 750 cc Indians and Harley-Davidsons. BSA's share was a third place for Albert Gunter in the 100-miler.

When, after missing out for 1950, the Motor-cycle Show reopened at Earls Court there was a grand display of machinery but, as the manufacturers had predicted, very little novelty. What few innovations there were — for example road-ster Nortons with Featherbed frames — were mostly ticketed 'for export only'. However, as the year was ending BSA announced 500 cc Gold Stars with new cylinder heads carrying bolted-on, die-cast rocker boxes. The barrels could be either sand- or die-cast, the obvious difference being that in the latter case the Piled Arms insignia on the pushrod tunnel was in relief instead of being engraved.

1952

Traditionally the sporting calendar's curtain raiser, the Colmore Cup trial had been demoted from trade-supported status, following an organisational breakdown in 1951, and it was the Victory trial that opened the season — with a surprise win for B. W. Martin (350 BSA). Thus did curly-headed, friendly, ever-cheerful Brian Martin begin his long and honourable career as a Small Heath works rider and an involvement with BSA that lasted for the rest of the company's life. He had already spent two seasons as Bill Howard's passenger and had figured in the class-awards lists of several trials, riding Francis-Barnett and BSA Bantam lightweights. His Victory win was especially fortuitous because he had just been promoted to the team to replace Johnny Draper, who had transferred to Nortons; and Nicholson, Tye and Martin won the team prize.

As their chief jockey at Daytona, BSA supported Canadian Billy Mathews, a much experienced Beach racer. But, having been out of action for two years, he was not on form and crashed in the Experts event. Of the numerous Gold Star riders, Albert Gunter finished fifth and Eugene Thiessen made the day's fastest lap.

A few weeks later Gene Thiessen was the hero in a World record speed attack mounted by BSA's independent distributor for the Pacific Coast area, Californian Hap Alzina. The famous Bonneville Salt Flats in Utah were used and two machines were prepared in Alzina's Oakland workshops. One was a 496 cc A7 Star Twin which, running under the American Motorcycle Association's Class C rules, had to be in standard catalogue trim, with a compression ratio of 8:1 for 80-octane fuel. After meticulous fettling it produced over 40 bhp on the bench, and Thiessen's average speed over two opposite-direction flying-mile runs worked out at 123.69 mph.

The second machine was a 646 cc A10 twin which, under Class A rules, was not so restricted as to specification. Tuned for a 90% methanol, 10% benzole fuel, it developed 60 bhp and carried no form of streamlining. Almost naked himself — he wore only tights, tennis shoes and goggles — Gene raised the flying-mile record to 143.5 mph.

In good time for the Isle of Man, a modified 350 Gold Star was made available in April. Retaining the 71 × 88 mm measurements, the unit had a strengthened main-bearing assembly and quieter cams. The rockers were unchanged but they were mounted in a one-piece die-casting secured to the Y-alloy, sand-cast cylinder head by nine studs. Larger diameter valves were inclined at 33 deg, instead of 37 deg, and the big-bore Amal TT carburettor had a steeper downdraught. The method of uniting head and barrel by four long and four short bolts was unchanged but the con rod was shortened by half an inch and the solid skirt of the die-cast piston was suitably abbreviated. For 'pool' petrol, the CR was 7.8:1. Die cast in Y-alloy, with an Austenitic iron liner, the barrel was shortened by 11/32 inch and had one less fin. The effect of these changes was immediate, as the Clubman's TT results showed (see Appendix A).

Nicholson was again at the top of the Trials Drivers Star league and Avery headed the Scramblers. He was also placed third (to Belgians Leloup and Mingels) in the newly inaugurated European Moto-cross Championship. And, for the umpteenth time, Harold Tozer was the British Expert sidecar driver.

It was a bleak year for Britain in the Austrian-based ISDT, but a trio of individualists emerged unscathed from the trial to complete an ambitious observed test. The riders were Fred Rist, Brian Martin and a young Birmingham clubman, Norman Vanhouse, just recruited to the BSA sales staff. Their machines were completely standard stock A7 Star Twins.

Under continual ACU supervision, the twins were ridden from Birmingham through London to Harwich and from The Hague via Paris, Geneva, Zurich and Innsbruck to Vienna. They came through the Six Days event without sacrificing a single mark and set off on a northward trek, taking a week to travel through Germany and Holland to Copenhagen, Malmo, Gothenburg and Oslo, where the test ended after 4,900 miles of motoring embracing calls at major cities and capitals in ten countries. Including the International week, the test had occupied 17 days of continuous riding without any mechanical breakdown, and when ACU observer John McNulty signed his report it was the last day on which entries for the Maudes Trophy competition could be accepted for the 1951-2 season. As there had not been any other entry for the 'Maudes' since 1939 it was pretty certain that BSA would have the Trophy on their stand at Earls Court. And they did.

Also on display at the Show were Gold Stars with new duplex cradle frames and pivoted-fork rear suspension. These BB types were the production editions of the models ridden by Ellis, Martin and Tye in the ISDT (all gold medal winners) and were, in fact, direct copies of a mount that Bill Nicholson had made for his own use. New also was the gearbox — an A7 unit shorn of the bolt-to-crankcase plate and provided with lugs for pivot mounting and adjustment in the usual separate box manner.

1953

A return, after 13 years absence, of premium-grade, brand-named petrol was a new year present for Britain's motorists, and another return, following a season's truancy, was that of Johnny Draper to the BSA competitions fold, which was further strengthened by the acquisition of the wonder-boy, Jeff Smith. Harold Tozer's retirement, to devote himself full-time to his growing motor-cycle business, was a blow but, fortunately, a new sidecar star with BSA affinities was in the ascendant — Frank Darrieulat, who won the first of the 1953 open events, the 'chairs only' D. K. Mansell trial.

Draper won the Victory, Smith the Alan Trophy, and Tye, Draper and E. P. Gill took the team prize in the Hurst Cup while Nicholson and Ellis were away on the Continent notching first and second places in Belgium's important Lamborelle trial. With further best performances, among them the Bemrose and Travers trials, Smith ended his first year with Small Heath atop the Star contest, and Draper was the solo British Expert. The Scramblers' competition saw Tye, Avery, Draper and Nex, in that order, behind Geoff Ward (AJS), with two new Beesa crossmen, D. G. Curtis and J. K. Hirst, eighth and tenth. In the Moto-cross Championship, Hall and Nex were fourth and seventh.

At Daytona Nick Nicholson (no relation to Bill) won a 50-mile race on a 500 Gold Star but in the longer events the Piled Arms collapsed.

With petrol rationing remaining in force for so long after the war, there had been a lively market for fuel-miserly little auxiliary power units, generally called 'clip-ons' and designed for attachment to pedal cycles. Rather tardily, BSA entered this field in May 1953 with a device named the Winged Wheel cyclemotor. Combined with a large-diameter drum hub in a normal bicycle wheel was a 35 cc two-stroke engine, complete with carburettor, flywheel magneto-generator, reduction gearing to an Eadie coaster freewheel, an internal-expanding brake and a clutch. Without need for any modifications, it took the place of the cycle's back wheel. Petrol-oil mixture was supplied from a box-shaped tank forming a bolt-on carrier. Producing about 1 bhp, with a fuel consumption of 200 mpg, the unit cost £25 (no purchase tax was required) and, although bearing BSA's 'winged B' symbol, it was made in the New Hudson Ltd Waverley works, a separate Small Heath factory in nearby Coventry Road.

BSA Motor Cycles Ltd and BSA Cycles Ltd were now individual companies operating under Armoury Road control, with George Savage as home sales manager and Bill Rawson in charge of exports. Sunbeams and Bantams were built in the Redditch plant, where Allan Jones was works manager.

A newly created post, that of press relations officer for BSA motor-cycle operations, was filled by R. C. E. Dancer, formerly a sub-editor with the *Birmingham Evening Mail*. With his professional ability Reg Dancer combined real enthusiasm for motor cycling and quickly won the confidence and respect of the Press Corps. He took an especial interest in assisting the Gold Star moto-cross teams, generally organising their forays at home and abroad and acting as their guide and counsellor. Through 20 years with BSA, latterly as PRO for the whole group, Reg maintained his high standards as a friendly source of fair, reliable news concerning his company's fluctuating fortunes.

1954

BSA's basic 1954 range contained 18 distinct types of motor cycles, plus the Winged Wheel auxiliary unit, the Sunbeams and the New Hudson autocycles. Newcomers were the D3 Bantam Major, with a 57 × 58 mm, 146 cc, engine; redesigned and lightened editions of the 249 cc sv and ohv mounts, now known as the C10L and C11G; and an A7 twin with an alloy cylinder head and swinging fork suspension that was listed, initially for export only, as the Shooting Star. With options of rigid, plunger and pivot-fork frames and alternative ignition systems, there were, in fact, 29 different BSA motor cycles in the catalogue, with prices, including Purchase Tax, from just over £80 for the D1 Bantam to £240 for the 500 Gold Star.

Additions to the competitions strength were Rex Young, whose trials reputation had been made on Nortons, and one of the best scramblers of the day, lanky, long-limbed Brian Stonebridge, a capture from the AMC Plumstead camp, to which flag Dave Curtis had reverted.

In the design department Bert Hopwood had been busy revising the Gold Stars, with a particular eye on the Daytona races. In the Experts 200-mile event, however, a pair of Star Twins

Opposite: Gold Star engines were approaching the peak of their development when this CB type was introduced in 1954 with eccentric rocker-spindle valve adjustment, extra-deep finning and a racing carburettor (Motor Cycle).

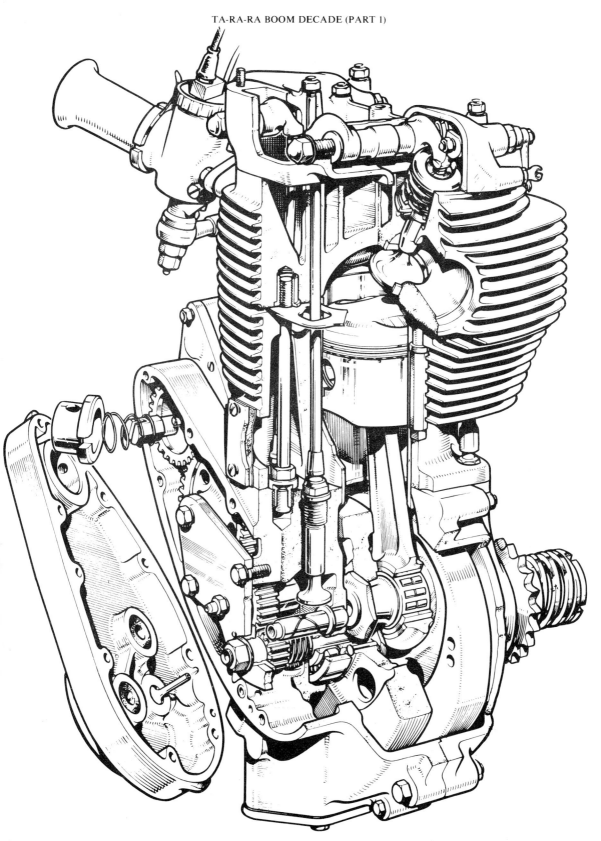

took the 1-2 honours, the riders being Bobby Hill and Dick Klamfoth, the latter an ex-Norton man with three previous victories to his credit. New Goldies, ridden by McDermott, Gunter, Ken Eggers and Warren Sherwood were third, fourth, fifth and eighth and the first nine places were all filled by British machines. Having thus convincingly proved the product, BSA announced the latest Gold Stars in April — 'with specifications suitable for all types of sport, from road racing to trials, and also for touring'.

The CB type mounts that immediately went into the hands of Clubman's TT entrants had massive alloy cylinder barrels with square-shaped fins surrounding the pushrod tunnels. The dimensions of 71 × 88 mm, 349 cc, and 85 × 88 mm, 499 cc, had not been changed but shortened con rods reduced overall engine height. Stronger crankpins and main bearing assemblies were incorporated to cope with extra power which, in a typical 500 racing engine, reached 37 bhp at 6,200 rpm (certificates detailing bench-test performances were issued with all these engines). A major break from tradition was the jettisonning of 'nut-and-bolt' tappet adjustment in favour of eccentrically mounted rocker spindles, allowing quick and accurate setting of valve clearances at rocker-box level. The ball-ended pushrods (actually light alloy tubes), located with cups on the tappet heads and rocker arms, and the valve angles were, inlet, 33 deg 45 min and, exhaust, 33 deg. They operated in heat treated, Y-alloy heads with oblique, vertical fins across the tops.

Because of the shorter con rod the flywheels of the bigger engines were machined slightly oval to clear the piston-skirt at bottom dead centre. To allay any misgivings that this unusual practice might arouse, BSA carefully pointed out that a rotating flywheel mass need not necessarily be circular (many two-stroke engines were balanced only by bob weights) and if properly balanced, ovality was perfectly satisfactory. A sleeve-valve crankcase breather working in the timing case, an Amal GP carburettor and needle-roller gearbox bearings were further novelties for the CB-type Goldies which, in Clubman's racing form, were fitted with clip-on handlebars.

As both BB and CB models were produced throughout the year, in 350 and 500 cc sizes, and with wide ranging racing, scrambling, trials and touring specifications, Gold Star customers had

plenty of options. In the Isle of Man, Beesas abounded; there were 54 in the Clubman's and 12 in the International races. Not since the unfortunate 1921 Senior had there ever before been more than three BSAs in a pukka TT.

So, after a long and patient process of development, BSA had launched a genuine, purpose-built racing motor cycle, and they sent a large team of factory personnel to the Island to minister to the needs of their riders. Among these backers-up was a new competitions manager, Dennis Hardwicke, a Londoner who had for five years been *Motor Cycling's* Midlands editorial man. Dennis had taken the job when Bert Perrigo, having held it for 22 success-filled years, moved to Selly Oak to join the Ariel administrative staff.

Returning in June from a Canada and US business trip, James Leek revealed that BSA had acquired the property and goodwill of Rich Child Inc, for many years Small Heath's East Coast distributors. Alf Rich Child had decided to retire after 33 years in the motor-cycle trade. The new president of the BSA-owned sales, spares, service and school organisation at Nutley, New Jersey, was Theodore 'Ted' Hodgden, a former executive at the Indian factory in Springfield, Mass. West Coast operations would continue in the hands of Hap Alzina.

In August Bill Nicholson departed to Coventry to join the development department at Jaguar cars, but he retained works support from Small Heath for trials and scrambles. Indeed he was the best soloist in the British Experts trial, with Jeff Smith second and Tom Ellis third. And Frank Darrieulat took Harold Tozer's erstwhile 'monopoly', the sidecar prize. In five years Billy Nicholson had twice won the solo Trials Drivers Star, twice taken the Scott Trial and twice been the solo British Expert.

During the trials season Jeff Smith had won four of the trade-supported open events and was four times a runner-up, so he easily headed the solo Star table. Furthermore, he tied for third place in the European Moto-cross Championship, just ahead of Stonebridge and Nex, who also tied. The Scrambles Star contest resulted in a decisive win for Geoff Ward, now back with AMC, but behind him came a string of seven BSA lads, led by Nex and including an up-and-coming Gold Star privateer, Terry Cheshire.

Chapter 17

Ta-ra-ra boom decade (Part 2)

'Now! Now!' cried the Queen. 'Faster! Faster!' — *Lewis Carroll*

1955

No important changes were made to the existing models. The 500 Star Twin was dropped and the Shooting Star was put on the home market. Also becoming available to British buyers during the year was a hitherto export-only, souped-up edition of the A10 Golden Flash, called the Road Rocket. Its 646 cc engine had an alloy head, a CR of 8:1 and an output of 40 bhp at 6,000 rpm. In readiness for the Isle of Man, the Clubman's Gold Stars (DB models) were given better, alloy-finned brakes, stronger carburettor mounting, swept-back exhaust pipes and sundry 'rider-comfort' modifications. Shorter piston skirts allowed the 500 cc engines to revert to circular flywheels. Rumours of a BSA scooter did not materialise, and Dennis Hardwicke made only one addition to the list of factory and factory-supported competitions riders, George Pickering, who had had many trials successes, especially on Bantam models, joining Avery, Draper, Ellis, Hall, Martin, Nex, Nicholson, Smith, Stonebridge, Tye and Young. Although not actually 'on the strength', several Continental BSA adherents, notably the hard-riding Swedish crossmen Bill Nilsson and Sten Lundin, could rely on Small Heath assistance.

The trials season began with Draper and Smith first and second in the Colmore Cup, and a month later Smith, Martin and Nicholson took the Victory team prize, Smith winning the trophy for the second year running. In March there was no joy for BSA at Daytona, their head lads Bobby Hill and Dick Klamfoth retiring from good positions in the Experts race.

In winning the premier award in the Scottish Six Days trial, Jeff Smith had a hard tussle on his hands for his 500 Gold Star was persistently chased by two machines of smaller capacity. At the end only two marks separated the leading trio — Smith, 20; G. E. Fisher (201 Francis-Barnett), 21; Gordon Jackson (350 AJS), 22. With the benefit of over 20 years hindsight it may be truly said that George Fisher was the man who first started to twitch the rug from under the entrenched dominance of the British 'big banger' ohv trials mount. Until his advent to the scene (he had also been runner-up in 1954) no one had

ever believed that a 'tiddler' two-stroke stood any chance in a major enduro like the 'Scottish'.

Held for the first, and only, time on the 10.8-mile Clypse Course, the Clubman's TT was overwhelmed with BSAs — only four out of 45 Junior entrants were on other makes. The Senior is particularly memorable for the clear-cut win by Eddie Dow. As Captain E. W. Dow, RASC, this perfervid BSA enthusiast had gained a high reputation as a gold-medal winner in Army ISDT teams before he made the 1953 Clubman's his first road race. In that event he crashed heavily after establishing a spectacular lead. A duff motor kept him out of the picture in the 1954 race, but on the Clypse circuit he fully confirmed his earlier promise as a road racer of exceptional ability, winning with well over a minute to spare. From then on Dow and BSA became synonymous names for not only did Eddie gain many more track successes, but he also went into business at Banbury, Oxfordshire, as a Gold Star specialist, preparing machines for private owners and marketing a wide variety of accessories. Dow's 'Goldie goodies' were prized by customers all over the world.

Returning from his Island victory, he teamed with Manxman Eddie Crooks to share a 500 Gold Star in the first experimental Thruxton 9-hours race for production machines. The two Eddies between them covered 221 laps of the Hampshire airfield circuit, winning by one lap from Ken James and Ivor Lloyd, whose mount was a 350 Goldie.

James Dickinson, works director of the Small Heath group, retired in June, after 40 years' service with BSA, and Bert Hopwood was appointed chief engineer of the Birmingham works. He had been chief designer for the previous six years. A month later, on Allan Jones becoming a director, Ernest E. Thompson, works manager at BSA's Dowlais, South Wales, factory, moved to a similar appointment at Redditch. At the same time BSA absorbed financial control of the Idoson Motor Cylinder Company, makers of motor vehicle cylinders since the war. Continuing as managing director was Harry Taft, member of one of the Midlands' best known motor-cycling families.

When the new season's models received their pre-Show publicity, BSA explained a pruning of the range to 11 basic machines by claiming that they needed more factory floor-space for manufacturing increased quantities of the types most in demand, and for developing new projects 'hitherto crowded out by the vastness of each year's production programme'.

In fact, not much pruning had really been done. That reliable old friend the 500 sv M20 was given the *coup de grâce*, as was the C11G, but the latter was replaced by a new 250 ohv C12 with an open frame, swinging rear fork and a new four-speed gearbox. The D3 Bantam had a cradle frame with pivot fork. Indeed, all the models had some form of rear suspension, and full-width hubs; some had chaincases, including the Road Rocket which was still for export only. There were no details of Gold Star changes, these being customarily announced in the following spring.

The real reason for the need for extra floor-space was revealed at the Show, in the form of two scooters, both of most unusual design. The larger of the pair, called the Beeza, had a 197 cc single-cylinder sv engine laid flat across a beam-type frame and driving through a single-plate clutch and four-speed box via a propeller shaft to a pinion and crown-wheel rear-axle assembly. The complete unit pivoted on a single bearing welded to the chassis and was controlled by a coil spring with separate Girling dampers. Multi-coil hairpin springs were used on the leading-link front fork and among other interesting features were a split big-end, 12-inch diameter perforated disc wheels and an electric starter. The Beeza embodied much that was basically 'car practice' in its make-up; it was priced at £165, plus £39 12s tax.

Perhaps more properly called a 'scooterette', was the Dandy 70. Here, a boomerang-shaped main frame composed of two welded-together steel pressings supplied the pivot mounting for an engine-clutch-integral-gear unit that swung with a pressed steel fork, one leg of which enclosed the driving chain. Spring struts regulated the movement. The 70 cc two-stroke engine had its single, horizontal cylinder pointing rearwards, outside the fork. A simplified version of the Beeza front fork was used; a kind of preselector mechanism, combined with the clutch, operated the two speeds; the 15-inch diameter wheels were wire spoked; and a wide frontal apron gave good leg protection. The price was £60 with £14 8s tax.

Technical journalists were unanimous in hailing BSA's entry into the scooter world as 'probably the boldest production venture ever to emanate from Small Heath'. Unfortunately, it came rather late in the day, for by this time the Continentals had enjoyed 10 years of virtually unopposed dominance in the scooter class and their stranglehold was hard to break.

On the sporting side, 1955 was unquestionably Jeff Smith's *annus mirabilis*. In addition to his 'Scottish' success, he had gone through the season like a whirlwind, riding his Gold Stars with brilliance in a host of trials and scrambles at home and abroad so that, when the year ended, his scorecard read: Head of the Scrambles Star contest with 36 points, two ahead of Terry Cheshire; winner of the Moto-cross des Nations; with three rides in a possible eight events he was seventh in the European Moto-cross Championship which was won by Draper with the Swedish BSA men Nilsson and Lundin second and third; in the Trials Drivers Star league he contested 15 of 32 events, winning four and finishing up in second place only five points behind AMC's Gordon Jackson who had had 16 rides; finally he won the British Experts trial in which Johnny Draper and Brian Martin were second and third.

And Jeffrey Vincent Smith was not yet 21!

1956

In May, Herbert Hopwood left for a board appointment with Norton Motors, after seven years with BSA during which he had launched the A10 models, vastly improved the Gold Stars and produced the Beeza and Dandy scooters, which were entirely his own brain-children. With him to Bracebridge Street went one of his principal lieutenants, Doug Hele. Remaining at Small Heath to take over design duties was Ernest Webster, who had assisted Hopwood throughout the scooter project.

Also left in Armoury Road was a unique design for a racing engine that BSA and Hopwood had earlier patented. Apart from having an outside flywheel, the bottom half of the single cylinder unit was conventional. The novelty lay in the operation of four radial overhead valves by a pair of short, bevel-geared camshafts set in a wide-angle, inverted-V athwart the cylinder head. Bevels and a vertical shaft took the drive from the mainshaft to one of the camshafts, which, in turn, drove the other. Pairs of rockers, on two similarly angled spindles, actuated the valves. Whether the performance of the Hopwood dohc motor would have justified the expense of its construction we shall never know, for it remains one of those imponderable 'models that might have been'. A 250 cc prototype, intended for use by Geoff Duke, was built but never raced.

Frederick William Hulse, former Small Heath general manager, died in mid-May, aged 72, and almost immediately there followed the revelation that Sir Bernard Docker had been dismissed from the board of directors and that his place as chairman of the 25-company BSA conglomerate would be taken by Jack Sangster. Sir Bernard did not give up his chairmanship without a fight. At a 3½-hour meeting of shareholders held at Grosvenor House in August, he tabled a motion of censure on the grounds that he had been summarily dismissed without proper reference to the shareholders. It was defeated by 365 votes to 118, and a further motion to remove Jack Sangster from office was also lost, by 303 to 109 votes. On a resolution proposed by Sangster, the meeting signified confidence in the board and approved its actions by 240 votes to 51.

A new Automotive Division of BSA Ltd was formed, including Daimler cars, Ariel, BSA, Sunbeam and Triumph motor cycles, with Edward Turner, already managing director of Triumph, as the managing director.

As chief executive, Edward Turner succeeded James Leek, CBE, who retired in September after some 46 years of distinguished service with the group. On leaving Newport Grammar School Jimmy Leek had been an engineering pupil at the Daimler, Coventry works before he moved to Small Heath's planning office, eventually becoming a BSA parent board director and managing director of the Small Heath and Daimler group of companies. His entry in *Who's Who* reads: '. . . latterly director BSA Ltd, BSA Guns Ltd, BSA Motor Cycles Ltd, Ariel Motors Ltd, Monochrome Ltd, Triumph Engineering Co Ltd; b. 1892.' He now lives at Stratford-on-Avon.

A major consequence of the formation of the Automotive Division was the departure from Armoury Road of the company's long established pedal cycle business. BSA Cycles Ltd was sold to Raleigh Industries, and with it to Nottingham went its sales director, Stan Digby. About the same time Sunbeam Motor Cycles Ltd and New Hudson Auto Cycles Ltd were registered as individual companies. And Bert Perrigo returned from Ariel to Small Heath as chief development engineer.

While the upheavals at management level were taking place, there was also 'trouble at t'mill'.

Much delay had been encountered in getting the two new scooters into production. The Dandy 70 models did not reach the market until October and, when the Show arrived in November, there was no Beeza: '. . . because it is now considered that the model may be uncompetitive in price in overseas markets it has been decided to review the whole project. For that reason the Beeza will not go into production as intended'. It never did, and the only example of this luxury concept that the public ever saw was the prototype displayed at the 1955 Show. However, the new season's range, not much altered, included for home sale the powerful and exotic Road Rocket, at £270 with tax. Press-tested, it did 109 mph on a 4.53:1 top gear at 6,200 rpm.

The sporting year had seen the last of the Clubman's TT races — swamped with BSA's and a double victory for Lincolnshire man, Bernard Codd. His 500 Gold Star was of the latest DBD type which, with a revised cylinder head, had come into being under the guidance of the Small Heath raceshop chief, Roland Pike, one of those rider-engineers whose enthusiasm for the sport was as much in the excitement of the chase as in the mechanics of producing a fast machine.

George Pickering had retired and Bill Nicholson and John Avery had 'semi-retired'; Jeff Smith, doing his National Service, had to limit his Continental moto-cross forays, but he won the Moto-cross des Nations. Using weekend leave passes to full advantage, he rode in eight of the 10 Scrambles Star events, topping the table 10 points ahead of the next man, Curtis (Matchless). Terry Cheshire was third and Dennis Hardwicke's valuable capture from the AMC ranks, Geoff Ward, was fourth. Except for Les Archer (Norton) in ninth place, all the remaining positions down to 12th were filled by BSA men.

Trials-wise, Smith won the British Experts for the second successive year and Frank Darrieulat, from Enfield, Middlesex, had his second win in the sidecar category. He also made best performance among the sidecars in the Trials Star contest.

The Pinhard Prize, instituted in memory of F. W. Pinhard, a notable Sunbeam MCC secretary, is awarded annually to an under-21 clubman who has made some outstanding contribution to motor-cycle sport. In 1956 it went to a Yorkshire youth named Arthur Lampkin whose excellent competitions season on a Gold Star had included the best-over-350 cc performance in the 'Scottish'. *Motor Cycling* remarked: 'His success has been one of sheer brilliance . . . Now a member of the BSA team, Lampkin seems set for a career of almost unparalleled success'. They could say that again . . . and again . . . and again!

With Christmas approaching, and Britain under Suez Crisis fuel rationing, BSA held their 95th annual general meeting, at which there was another attempt to remove Jack Sangster from the parent board. He, and John E. Rowe, ACA, the company's financial director for many years, both being due for retirement in rotation, had offered themselves for re-election. They were reinstated by votes of 36 to 27 and 32 to 22 respectively.

Reporting on the year's trading, Sangster referred to 'very severe losses' in the motorcar division, but motor-cycle sales, particularly exports, were being well maintained. Independent investigations into the group's affairs had revealed a need for some restructuring and reorganisation, especially at Small Heath, and 'the first aim of the board would be to strengthen those sections which had shown ability to make profits and to eliminate losses wherever they were made'.

The group's total, pre-tax profits that year amounted to £1,604,000.

1957

The year was barely a month old when Roland Pike, who for four years had been in charge of engine development, departed, via a short stay with the SU Carburettor company, for America. From there he contributed a lengthy article to *Motor Cycling* setting forth his practical proposals for building a racing 250 BSA, using such items as 'cut-down' Gold Star components and a Sunbeam S7 connecting rod. Engines based on 'Pike practices' were subsequently constructed and raced by several British enthusiasts. Pike's arrival in the States was not, however, made in time for him to see his Armoury Road-prepared machines perform in the Daytona Beach meeting, wherein the 100-mile Amateur event was won by Kenny Brown on a Gold Star and, on similar models, Albert Gunter and Gene Thiessen were second and third to a Harley-Davidson rider in the 200-mile Experts race.

After five years' management of the competitions department Dennis Hardwicke became BSA Motor Cycles' technical sales manager.

The Scottish Six Days trial was won by Royal Enfield's Johnny Brittain, after a needle fight with Jeff Smith, Johnny Draper and Arthur Lampkin, the BSA trio carrying off the team prize. Smith went on to win the British Moto-cross Grand Prix, and in the Thruxton Nine-hours race F. Webber and R. Davey, sharing a 350 Goldie, were the victors.

With the death on July 25 of Herbert Perkins, BSA lost one of their most experienced and respected engineers. Through 37 years in the design office he had initiated and assisted in the company's motor-cycle projects and had played a large part in the production of the BSA Scout car. Among his numerous contributions to machine-tool improvement was his design for a special kind of copy-turning lathe, much used in the group's workshops.

It was Great Britain's turn to host the autumn Moto-cross des Nations contest and, in front of a huge Brands Hatch crowd, the home side fielded Draper, Martin, Smith, Stonebridge and Derek Rickman, all on BSAs, and Dave Curtis (Matchless). Except for Italy, all the other competing nations — Belgium, Denmark, Holland and Sweden — had at least one BSA rider in their teams. Britain won the event and Jeff Smith made the best individual performance.

At the October annual general meeting Jack Sangster announced parent board changes. Retired directors were Sir Patrick Hannon, Sir Frank Smith and James Leek. Five new members had been appointed: two, Edward Turner and Robert P. Wallace, would be executives; the non-executive three were Sir James Reid Young. C. Godfrey Phillips and A. J. Quig. Robert Wallace had for two years been managing director of the BSA Steel Division, comprising William Jessop Ltd, J. J. Saville and Co Ltd, and Bromley, Fisher and Turton Ltd. With the present directors — Jack Sangster, Lewis Chapman, Noel Docker, H. P. Potts and J. E. Rowe — the board numbered ten, with an average age of 60. Chairman Sangster reported that profits for the past financial year showed an increase to £2,100,000 from £1,600,000 and a bank loan of £2,630,000 had been repaid. Dividends would be raised to ten per cent.

The group's improved trading position reflected the buoyant motor-cycle market — Board of Trade figures revealed that the month of July had hit an all-time record for British motor-cycle production, 21,840 machines. The previous highest total had been in May when the figures was 19,029.

Nevertheless, the nation had problems — the Suez Crisis, petrol rationing, increased purchase tax and a heavy credit squeeze. This, said the Manufacturers Union, was not the right time to hold a Motor Cycle Show; until things improved the Earls Court exhibition would be staged every other year. Had there been a Show, the BSA display would have been more noteworthy for the variety of its colour schemes than for any great novelty. Full-width hub brakes were fitted to all the ohv machines; the A7 and A10 twins had a revised crankshaft assembly embodying a sludge trap; rear chaincases and headlamp nacelles were available on many models.

The removal from the range of the 250 sv C10L left only one quarter-litre type, the C12 ohv; also, the dropping of the B32 Gold Star meant that the evergreen B31 was the sole representative in the 350 category; another casualty was the M33 ohv 591 cc machine. Its sv companion, the M21, continued as the only plunger-sprung type and the only model to which a BSA sidecar could be attached. B34 Gold Stars were offered in racing and scrambling trim but not to trials specification. Specially made for American rough riders was the Rocket Scrambler version of the 646 cc alloy-engined Super Rocket.

At the year's end Jeff Smith was declared the three-in-a-row solo winner of the British Experts trial, and Frank Darrieulat took the sidecar award. Four months later Smith was deprived of his title, following a protest by another rider.

Because petrol-rationing had caused the cancellation of many sporting events, the ACU Star awards were not made in 1957.

1958

Springtime personnel changes included the return to Small Heath of Bob Fearon. For the past two years he had been acting, from Coventry, as works director of both Triumph and BSA Motor Cycles and in May he transferred his office to Armoury Road to concentrate on BSA operations. Dennis Hardwicke was appointed chief of the group's accessory-making Metal and Plastics subsidiary.

Under the guidance of Bert Perrigo, Brian Martin assumed the 'gaffer's' duties in the 'comp shop' and the riders lined up for 1958 were, Martin, Ellis, Young, Smith, Draper, Lampkin, Rickman, Taft and Darrieulat. Taft was a BSA apprentice and Smith, now out of the Army and having entered his father's business, was not wholly committed to competitions. Brian Stonebridge had joined the Greeves concern and Terry Cheshire was riding Royal Enfields. Trials and scrambles rivalry at this period was intense and the experts from at least half a dozen factories were sharing the spoils, with a large proportion of the premier awards going to riders of 250 cc machines which had become the 'in thing' for sports wear.

BSA had no competitive production machine

Much clever design work went into the 249 cc ohv vertical-twin unit that powered the 1958 BSA Sunbeam scooter, which had an electric starter (Motor Cycle).

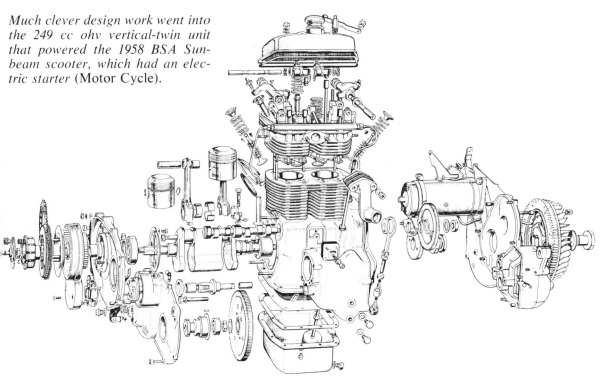

in this class until, in September, came the announcement of a completely new design for a 70 mph ohv 250 to replace the C12. Called the C15 250 Star, it had a 67 × 70 mm semi-high-camshaft engine in unit with a four-speed gear cluster and mounted in a single-down-tube cradle frame. An Amal Monobloc carburettor and a 50-watt Lucas AC generator were features and on a 7.25:1 compression ratio it produced 15 bhp at 7,000 rpm. The man behind this £172 package was Bert Perrigo and it was the highspot of the eight-basic-model range announced in October for 1959 sales. The D3 150 cc Bantam Major had been superseded by a 175 cc (61.5 × 58 mm) D5 Bantam Super and the sole remaining sidevalver, the M21, was virtually pensioned off, being available only to special order. And for the first time since 1913, there were no sidecars.

The only motor-cycle firm that had consistently made their own sidecars — bodywork as well as chassis — BSA had catered well for the 'combo' brigade, and their commodious, comfortable, well-made models had provided cheap and pleasant travel for countless families. But the individualistic crafts of joinery and upholstering did not fit in with the group's automotive concept and, except for a tiny section still making gun stocks, all signs of woodworking were swept from Armoury Road.

There were no Sunbeams, either. The unique, in-line twins had gone through a 12-year production run with practically no modifications whatever (surely a record for any kind of motor vehicle?) but rising prices and *anno domini* had overtaken them. Conceived as 'gentlemen's motor cycles', they had themselves become old gentlemen, somewhat short of puff but suave and courtly to the end.

The sporting fraternity had been expecting a 250 Gold Star, based on Terry Cheshire's 1956 ISDT gold-medal-winning prototype, but it did not materialise. Indeed, there never was such a thing as a production quarter-litre Goldie and it is a curious reflection that BSA, always so keen on reliability trials, did not have a single trials mount in their 1959 catalogue, although the new C15 Star was obviously in line for a competitions specification.

Kept as an 'eve of Show surprise' (although an open secret for many months) was the publication of details of a joint BSA-Triumph invasion of the scooter world. This was the first example of dual-role marketing (identical models carrying different brand names) to be adopted by the Automotive Division. Hitherto, the products of

Small Heath and Meriden had strictly maintained their separate, distinctive characteristics, following a policy that promoted healthy rivalry between the factories and encouraged zealous loyalties among the customers.

Coming from Edward Turner's Meriden design office were plans for a chassis-body layout that could accommodate engines of two different types, one a single-cylinder 175 cc two-stroke and the other a 250 cc ohv vertical twin. As BSA Sunbeams, they were listed as the models 175B1 and 250B2; the equivalent Triumph-labelled machines were the TS1 and TW2 Tigresses.

Engine-gearbox units were rigidly mounted upright under the dual seat in a frame consisting of two main tubes cross-braced by flat floor members. A combined chaincase-swinging arm assembly was controlled by a single hydraulically damped spring unit and an oblong, box-shaped 'fork' leg on the left side carried the front wheel. The disc wheels, being stub-axle mounted, were quickly detachable and interchangeable. Basic prices ranged from £132 to £161, and the twin models could be fitted with an electric starter at option.

The scooters were given a lavish coming-out party at Grosvenor House, attended by numerous personalities. The glamorous fashion girl, Barbara Goalen modelled the Tigress models and Harry Secombe lent his weight to the occasion, declaiming that he was 'wanted for a Sunbeam'. More seriously, Jack Sangster told the dealers that it was the group's intention 'to produce a thousand a week of the models now showing'. It proved an over-optimistic prophecy, for this second venture into the scooter world fared little better than the first.

In November Noel Docker, a cousin of Sir Bernard, resigned from the parent board.

Rumours of a revived 350 Gold Star were not founded but, in the last major sporting event of the year, the Southern Experts trial, Brian Martin and Jeff Smith were first and fifth on prototype trials versions of the 250 Star.

1959

Competition editions of the 250 Star model — the C15T and C15S trials and scrambles types — were in dealers showrooms by February, priced at £183 and £188 respectively. Developing nearly 20 bhp at 7,500 rpm, they were splendid performers, Smith, Martin, Draper, Lampkin & Co continuing to reap the same harvests of 'best solo' and team prizes as they had customarily garnered on their Goldies. A further indication of the growing popularity of smaller capacity engines was seen in the entry list for the Golden Jubilee Scottish Six Days trial — 107 of the 181 soloists choosing under 250 cc machines. In that notorious engine-wrecking, frame-breaking classic, the Scott Trial, Jeff Smith, with his C15T, not only won but set a new standard-time record.

Lampkin won the Scrambles Star competition and Darrieulat was second in the Trials Star sidecar section, wherein North-West London dealer W. C. 'Bill' Slocombe, placed fourth, began his long career as a consistent prize winner aboard his immaculately prepared BSA outfits.

There was no Earls Court Show, and the BSA range of motor cycles and scooters was carried forward unchanged into the 1960s. Fuel rationing was over. At a total of more than a million and a half, there had never been more machines on British roads, and exports, particularly to North America, were winning huge sums of valuable foreign currency. As it closed its books on the 'Fortunate Fifties' the industry felt it could justifiably expect the coming decade to send sales graphs soaring clean off the wallcharts.

There was, however, an omen. A rising sunspot had appeared in the east. Early in the year one of the technical journals had road-tested what was believed to be the first powered two-wheeler ever imported to the UK from Japan. The 250 cc Rabbit scooter, it was called, and it completely shattered the widely held belief that Japanese motor-cycle makers produced only crude copies of obsolete European machines, using bamboo for frames and lead shot for ball bearings. The Rabbit was made by a leading Nippon engineering concern, Fuji Heavy Industries, and it was not only very well made but possessed a number of ingeniously original features and had a performance that lacked nothing in comparison with its Western equivalents.

Surprise number two came with the arrival in the Isle of Man of a shipment of Japanese racing motor cycles, together with Japanese riders to handle them. The machines — Honda 125 cc ohc twins — were a revelation, and when their riders proceeded to tackle the tricky Clypse Course as though they had known it all their lives, the Occidental attitude to Oriental motor-cycle progress changed rapidly from patronising amusement to serious respect, not untinged by apprehension.

In the 125 cc Lightweight TT all four of the Japanese riders finished, in sixth, seventh, eighth and eleventh places, and the Honda Motor Co, at the first time of asking, won the makers' team prize in a field packed with the fastest Italian and German machinery in the hands of championship aces like Hailwood, Taveri, Provini and Ubbiali.

The sunspot that was ultimately to contribute to the total eclipse of the British motor-cycle industry had made its ominous impact.

Chapter 18

Winds of change

'How are the mighty fallen in the midst of battle!' — *2 Samuel i, 25*

Now in its 99th year, the BSA organisation moved smoothly into the 1960s full of optimism. At the head of affairs was Jack Sangster, a chairman of vast practical experience in whose commercial judgment shareholders and staff alike had every confidence. His lieutenants were mostly men who had long worked under him in the various group companies, and collectively they represented some of the best brains in the business.

Into this team, in the new year, came Eric Turner — no relation to the Edward of that ilk, but a 42-year-old qualified accountant who had previously been chairman of the Blackburn and General Aircraft company. He joined the parent board as chief executive of the group and succeeded the retiring Lewis Chapman as deputy chairman. At the same time a new management policy was introduced, intended to make the individual companies function autonomously. It applied to BSA Motor Cycles Ltd, Triumph Engineering Co Ltd, Ariel Motors Ltd, Idoson Motor Cylinder Co Ltd and Metal and Plastic Components Ltd. The BSA board consisted of Eric Turner, Bill Rawson, Allan Jones and J. W. Binsted (secretary).

On the sporting side there were two new recruits to the 'comp shop', J. L. Harris and J. F. Burton. John Harris was a trials and scrambles man with many successes in his five years of BSA riding. Son of former speedway star, Squib Burton, 'Big John' Burton, of Lutterworth, one of the strongest and most forceful of scramblers, had particularly distinguished himself as a member of the victorious British team in the 1959 Moto-cross des Nations battle. The official BSA competition riders for 1960 were, for trials: Johnny Draper, Jim Harris, Arthur Lampkin, Dave Langston, Brian Martin, Jeff Smith; for scrambles: Burton, Draper, Harris, Lampkin, Martin, Smith.

After the 'Scottish', in which Smith, Draper and Martin won the makers' team prize, all on 250 cc machines, a new BSA sidecar expert arose, Sam Seston, who had taken the best opposite-class award.

In readiness for showing at Earls Court was the model B40 350 Star, replacing the discon-tinued, long-loved B31. It had a short-stroke engine with a capacity quite novel for BSA, 343 cc (79 × 70 mm). Outwardly it bore a strong family resemblance to the 250 Star and was the only over-250 cc road-going single-cylinder mount in the range, the B33 499 cc type having also been dropped, along with the D5 150 cc Bantam Major. Only the D1 and D7 (125 and 173 cc) two-strokes were listed.

With 170,025 visitors, the Show had the best seven-day attendance since 1953 when the gate had totalled 187,096. One regular figure on the BSA stand was absent; David William Munro, who had served the company since 1920, had died in October. His post as technical liaison engineer was taken over by Arthur Lupton, whose explicit instruction books and service manuals are still in demand by BSA owners and restorers.

'Exactly one hundred years ago today, at a meeting in a Birmingham hotel room, it was decided to form The Birmingham Small Arms Company Limited'. So read the preface to the June 7 1961 Centenary Issue of *BSA Group News*. And in the same week Jack Sangster, having reached 65, retired as chairman, although remaining as a director. Reporting an all-time record profit of £3,418,000, 'Mister Jack' handed over to Eric Turner the control of an engineering enterprise embracing some 30 English-based companies, making everything from heavy machine tools to taxicab bodies, together with four transatlantic subsidiaries. They were listed as follows:

The Birmingham Small Arms Co Ltd
Head office: Armoury Road, Birmingham
London office: BSA House, St James's Street, SW1

Automotive Companies
Ariel Motors Ltd, Selly Oak, Birmingham. *Motor cycles*
BSA Motor Cycles Ltd, Small Heath, Birmingham. *Motor cycles and scooters*
Service and Spares Department, Waverley Works, Coventry Road, Birmingham. *Servicing BSA motor cycles, BSA and Triumph scooters and BSA power units*
BSA Power Unit Division, Redditch, Worcs. *Air-cooled*

64: *From the Golden Hillock end of Armoury Road, the great BSA works presented a bold front in 1965. As the sign on the centre block shows, it had already become the home of Ariel Motors, transferred from Selly Oak in 1963.*

65: *Demands from America for power, and yet more power, leading to the creation of the Superbike class, were met by BSA in 1966 by the rugged, unsilenced, twin-carb, alloy-engined production racer, the 650 cc Hornet.*

66: *(Left) BSA put their neat little ohv 250 cc engine to many uses in many frames. In this Victor 250 type it went across the Atlantic, in 1971, as a street-scrambler. With similar styling, but with a 499 cc engine, it was called the Gold Star 500.*

BSA VICTOR 250

67: *(Below) A street machine of another sort was the B25 250 cc Fleetstar, a 1970 bid to capture the market for light delivery service vehicles. The fittings were made by BSA's subsidiary Motoplas accessory company.*

B 25 FLEETSTAR

58: *With a finned cover over its light-alloy cylinder head, the 500 Royal Star was a well-equipped, medium-powered middleweight that made its debut in 1970.*

59: *There is no mistaking the intended destination for this exotic mount — the USA, of course. As the 650 Firebird Scrambler, it was another of Small Heath's offerings for customers calling for machines that combined maximum power with the latest fashion in ancillary equipment.*

70: *Britain's dramatic contribution to the 750cc Superbike class was the transverse ohv triple-cylinder unit designed by Bert Hopwood's BSA/Triumph team and made in two styles by BSA at Small Heath. The BSA Rocket-Three had inclined cylinders in a duplex loop frame; at first the Triumph Trident had an upright engine in a single-down-tube frame, but later models used the sloping unit. The Rocket-Three pictured has the polished alloy front fork, with two-way damping, introduced in 1971.*

71: *As the 1960s ended, the Bantam made its last appearance as the D14 Bushman, intended for rough country, forestry and general 'outback' duties. A trials version, built by Brian Martin's competitions team, could well have been Britain's answer to the foreign two-stroke invasion, but the 'comp shop' was closed before it got going.*

72: *Figuring in the last-ever BSA catalogue of 1972, the 650 cc, single-carburettor Thunderbolt twin had a large-diameter main frame tube that also served as an oil container.*

BSA LIGHTNING 650

73: (Left) The Lightning 650 was the twin-carburettor edition of the Thunderbolt (picture No 72). Both machines were lavishly equipped and had two-leading-shoe brakes, but an unfavourably high riding position resulted from the new frame design.

74: (Below) Armoury Road, 1977. Deserted and derelict, the New Building still stands, but at the far end of the famous street there is only open space, the original head-office block and surrounding workshops having entirely disappeared.

75: *As first produced in 1968, the BSA Rocket-Three was styled for the American market with fittings and embellishments such as cow-horn bars and an ornamental alloy oil-cooler cowling between the cylinder head and tank. It was not until April 1969 that the anglicised versions started to reach British customers.*

BSA FURY 350 SS 18

76: *(Left) Edward Turner designed the double overhead camshaft 350 cc parallel twin unit that was to power the BSA Fury SS (in Triumph livery it was named the Bandit). It was tooled up at great cost, but the Group's financial problems boiled over in 1971 and the project went into limbo before it had reached the production stage.*

77: *(Below) 'BSA will never die!' That is the warcry of the BSA Owners Club — more than 2,000 enthusiasts dedicated to preserving the marque's good name. Here a group of them gather for the prize-distribution ceremony at a 1976 camping weekend at Slimbridge in Gloucestershire.*

engines for industry and agriculture
Motoplas Company Ltd, Waverley Works, Coventry Road, Birmingham. *Motor cycle and scooter equipment and accessories; plastic mouldings*
Triumph Engineering Co Ltd, Meriden Works, Allesley, Coventry. *Motor cycles and scooters*

Tool Companies
Automation Jigs & Tools Ltd, Bath Road, Wolverhampton. *Engineering and design consultants*
BG Machinery Ltd, Montgomery Street, Sparkbrook, Birmingham. *Reconditioners of used machine tools*
BSA Broach Co Ltd, Redditch, Worcs. *Design and manufacture of broaching tools and fixtures*
BSA Small Tools Ltd, Montgomery Street, Sparkbrook, Birmingham. *Small tools and workshop equipment*
BSA Tools Ltd, Mackadown Lane, Kitts Green, Birmingham. *Machine tools and special purpose machines*
Burton, Griffiths & Co Ltd, Mackadown Lane, Kitts Green, Birmingham. *UK sales organisation for BSA tools and products of US and Continental manufacturers*
The Churchill Machine Tool Co Ltd, Altrincham, Cheshire. *Precision grinding machines*
Precision Alloy Castings (B'ham) Ltd, Mackadown Lane, Kitts Green, Birmingham. *Alloy steel castings*

Steel Companies
Jessop-Saville Ltd, Brightside Works, Sheffield. *Special steels and alloys; forgings and castings; titanium and zirconium*
Jessop-Saville (Small Tools) Ltd, Rotherham, Yorks. *Tungsten carbide tool tips, finished tools and wear-resisting parts; high speed steel tools*

Small Arms
BSA Guns Ltd, Shirley, Solihull, Warwicks. Also: Dowlais, Merthyr Tydfil, Glamorgan. *Air rifles, shot guns, hunting rifles, match rifles and military arms*

General Engineering
BSA Metal Powders Ltd, Montgomery Street, Sparkbrook, Birmingham. *Pre-alloyed metal powders*
BSA Precision Castings, Redditch, Worcs. *Investment castings; high-definition sand castings; sand shell-moulded castings*
Birtley Engineering Ltd, Birtley, Co Durham. Also: Chesterfield, Derbyshire. *Coal preparation plant and materials handling equipment*
Carbodies Ltd, Coventry. *Motor vehicle bodies, general presswork and sheet metal fabrication*
Idoson Motor Cylinder Co Ltd, Tividale, Tipton, Staffs. *Air-cooled cylinder castings; repetition castings; shell-moulded castings*
Metal & Plastic Components Ltd, Montgomery Street, Sparkbrook, Birmingham. *Production of components by powder metallurgy*
Monochrome Ltd, Redditch, Worcs. *Industrial plating*

Research Establishments
Group Research Centre, Mackadown Lane, Kitts Green, Birmingham. *Serving the Group as a whole*
Whiston Grange Research Laboratories, Rotherham, Yorks. *Research for steel companies*

Overseas Subsidiaries
BSA Incorporated, USA
BSA Tools (Canada) Ltd
Jessop-Saville (Canada) Ltd
The Triumph Corporation, USA

Amidst the centennial celebrations Bert Hopwood returned from Norton to the Automotive Division as a director and general manager of the Triumph company at Coventry. Arthur Lampkin's brother Alan and Bryan Povey joined the competitions squad and, following the death after the Colmore trial of Sam Seston, Bill Slocombe became BSA's sidecar expert. On the race tracks, an Armoury Road experimental shop engineer, Chris Vincent, began to make a reputation with an ultra-low sidecar outfit built by himself and powered by a BSA twin-cylinder engine. He won that season's ACU Sidecar Racing Star.

There was no Show in 1961 and the only new model introduced during the year was an 80 mph edition of the 250 cc C15 Star, the SS80 Sport Star which, apart from a smaller bore, shared its specification with the 343 cc B40 model.

However, 1962 was not a week old when BSA made two additions to the twin-cylinder range. These were the A50 and A65 Star Twins. Of new design, they differed chiefly from the long-standing A7, Shooting Star and Golden Flash types, which they quickly displaced, in having engine-gear unit construction (triplex-chain) and Lucas AC/DC 12-volt electrical equipment instead of the separate magneto and dynamo layout. Further engine design features included a one-piece, diecast light-alloy cylinder head with integral lugs to make a very rigid rocker assembly, neatly enclosed by a shallow, smooth-contoured cover. The engines shared a common stroke measurement of 74 mm, the bores being 65.5 and 75 mm, producing capacities of 499 and 654 cc. A redesigned, all-welded, duplex-loop frame with brazed-on engine lugs was evolved for the newcomers, Girling spring units and floating brake shoes being also featured.

In February came a high-performance hybrid, the Rocket Gold Star, resulting from a marriage of the 46 bhp engine from the Super Rocket with the race-bred Gold Star frame. Both the parent models remained unchanged although Goldies were offered in limited quantities only, either to scrambles specification or in clubman's trim with a wide range of additional equipment for road racing. Although it was still possible, for another couple of seasons, to obtain DBD-type B34s, on special order, after 1962 Gold Stars disappeared from the catalogues, much to the sorrow of the many friends they had made during their near quarter-century of production.

The group said goodbye to another of the 'class of 1920' stalwarts when Noel Brearley retired in January 1962; his position as advertising manager was filled by Ivor Davies, who had been in charge of the Triumph publicity office since his demobilisation after the Second World War. One of his first jobs at Small Heath was to advertise BSA's first, and only, capture of an International Tourist Trophy. This one-off, out-of-the-blue success came when Chris Vincent, aided by his printer passenger, Eric Bliss, rang up three impressive Island firsts with their 'home-built', privately entered 497 cc BSA twin/Watsonian outfit — (1) In beating all the BMW experts, including Max Deubel and Florian Camathias, they became the first all-British crew to win a Sidecar TT since 1954; (2) Theirs was the first Mountain Course British sidecar victory since 1925; (3) Their machine had the first push-rod engine to win an International TT since 1936 — a distinction that still stands. Vincent averaged 83.57 mph over the three laps and among the 13 finishers were three other BSA outfits. Before retiring, Deubel had made the first over-90 mph (90.7 mph) lap in a Sidecar TT.

A mid-season introduction was a Sport Star edition of the 343 cc B40, the SS90. Not content with a 14-model range of motor cycles, plus three scooters (the Sunbeams were still being made, but the Dandy 70 had been dropped), the group made a combined BSA/Ariel bid for the ultra-lightweight market, staging an eve-of-Show display of two lively little ones with ohv engines outwardly alike but of different capacities and mounted in quite different swing-fork frames.

The BSA version was the Beagle, whose 75 cc (47.6 × 42 mm) four-speed unit-construction motor was hung in a welded pressed-steel chassis. With a frame reminiscent of their Leader and Arrow motor cycles, Ariel presented the 50 cc Pixie model. A 50 mph job, the Beagle's all-in price was £92 10s.

Both engine designs emanated from Edward Turner's drawing office and the Pixie, much to the chagrin of the Selly Oak people, was 'wished' on them just as they were completing, unbeknown to Turner, a most promising model of their own. This had a 175 cc engine whose overhead camshaft was driven by a toothed rubber belt — for those days a highly advanced idea adopted by Ariel's director and general manager, K. J. Whistance. A former New Imperial executive who had raced in the TT, Ken Whistance was bitterly disappointed when Turner vetoed the ohc engine and replaced it with the smaller version of the Beagle unit.

Ariel suffered another blow when, in March 1963, they were bundled out of their ancestral Selly Oak home and transferred to Armoury Road, Ken Whistance being appointed to the BSA Motor Cycles board as general development director.

At the end of the year Edward Turner, although continuing as a member of the parent board, relinquished his managing directorships, at his own request, and handed over to H. G. Sturgeon who, like Eric Turner, had previously been engaged in the aircraft industry. A capable businessman, Harry Sturgeon, after leaving the De Havilland company at Hatfield, had for a while been managing director of the BSA subsidiary, The Churchill Machine Tool company. From Altrincham, he came to Small Heath and, with Bert Hopwood as second in command, and with John Balder, OBE, as director of production planning, set to work with enthusiasm as managing director of the group's motor-cycle division. Sadly, his reign was short, for he died within three years of his appointment.

Jeff Smith won his third British Experts trial, rounding off another year of magnificent riding; but he lost his factory team-mates John Burton and John Harris, who had not been happy with their current competition models, which were 'light 500s' of 420 cc. They quit their jobs at Armoury Road to ride Matchless-Metisse scramblers which they felt gave them a better chance in the 500 cc moto-cross class. Concurrently, Arthur Lampkin (whose brother Alan had been doing well on 250 cc BSAs), with an eye on the lightweight category, signed up to ride Villiers-engined Cottons, thus foreseeing, and mightily helping to bring about the small-capacity two-stroke machines' ultimate overthrow of the traditional 'big bangers'. He did not, however, entirely abandon his BSA connection and, in the years when scrambling was an important feature of television sports programmes, Arthur, on his Small Heath four-strokes, became a notable small-screen star.

The 420 cc single-cylinder types were developed into the very much more competitive B41 441 cc Victor and Victor Special models and it was on machines of this pattern that those two mighty moto-crossmen John Banks and (for a brief period) Vic Eastwood teamed with Smith and Lampkin in many a televised rough and tumble.

Through the middle and late 1960s BSA's motor-cycle division sailed on seemingly smooth waters, and for their export achievements Small Heath and Meriden were both granted the Queen's Award for Industry in 1967 and again in 1968. There were, however, all manner of diversions taking place within the group's non-motor-cycle ramifications. In 1966 the whole of the Tools Division was sold to the famous Alfred

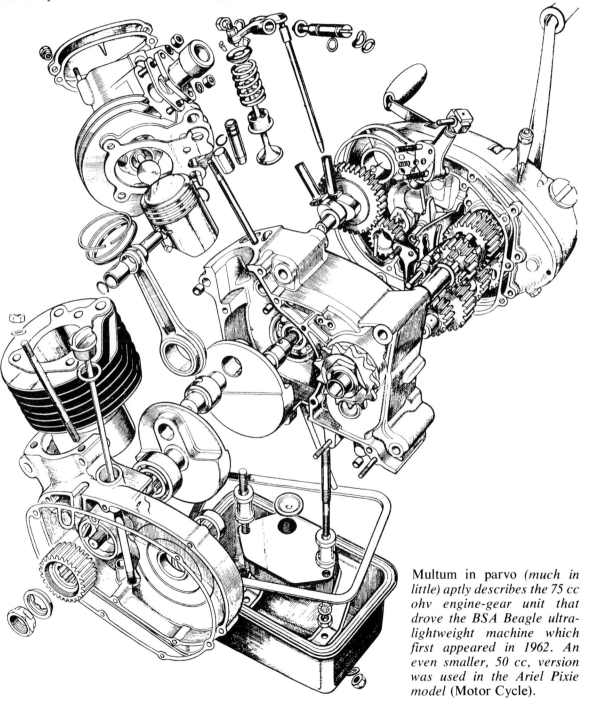

Multum in parvo (*much in little*) *aptly describes the 75 cc ohv engine-gear unit that drove the BSA Beagle ultra-lightweight machine which first appeared in 1962. An even smaller, 50 cc, version was used in the Ariel Pixie model* (Motor Cycle).

Herbert company, a deal that went sour because payment had been accepted in Herbert shares which, when later turned into cash, cost BSA several million pounds. A year later the steel-making subsidiary, Jessop-Saville was bought by Firth-Brown and the J-S titanium business went to Imperial Metal Industries; the accruing £5½ million was not rated as a good bargain for Small Heath. Thereafter, a series of acquisitions, disposals and mergers followed, linking BSA with such organisations as SMC Sterling Ltd, Tube Investments and the British Steel Corporation.

A man from outside the motor-cycle industry, Lionel Jofeh, succeeded to Harry Sturgeon's responsibilities in February 1967. One of his first actions was to establish a research and development 'think tank' at Umberslade Hall, a stately mansion set in acres of Warwickshire parkland near Solihull. Here a group of some 250 scientists and engineers researched freely, but came up with very little that helped with the development of motor cycles.

Up to this point motor-cycle sales had been brisk. In 1968 the BSA/Triumph combination was accounting for over 80 per cent of the industry's exports, but in that invaluable market, North America, where there was only one indigenous make, Harley-Davidson, there was widespread alarm among the importing dealers at the lack of British progress. Japanese and Continental makers had gained a monopoly of the lightweight field and the English heavyweights, despite States-style fittings and trimmings, were still fundamentally Golden Flashes, not only retaining the incurable vibration characteristics of a parallel-twin design, but aggravating them as capacities were progressively increased to meet the demands of the new, US-inspired superbike class.

Attempts to obtain smoother performance from the double-bore 'thumpers' by applying special, expensive techniques to machine-turned flywheels and more massive crank assemblies did not successfully solve the vibration problem, which became even more obtrusive when the Japanese began producing large-capacity, sweet-running, four-cylinder four-strokes and multi-cylinder two-strokes that were greeted with enthusiasm by American riders.

Since the retirement of Edward Turner, who had always kept in close personal touch with his companies' US salesmen, there had been a considerable redistribution of the group's American outlets and personnel. BSA Incorporated had been moved from Nutley to Verona, New Jersey, and, Hap Alzina having retired, distribution on the West Coast was now made from a centre at Duarte, California. On both sides of the States there was a feeling that contact with the English factories was deteriorating and, furthermore, that nothing was being done to counter the Japanese onslaught.

In the main, there was some justification for these recriminations. BSA management was preoccupied with diversifying the group's operations into spheres that had nothing to do with motor cycles, such as central heating, sintered metal production and powdered-iron foundry work, so that, as the end of the 1960s approached, the range of BSA motor cycles had been reduced to a mere handful of models.

Discontinuance of the four-speed D10 Bantam had left only one two-stroke machine in production, the D14 175 cc Bantam Super; a high-performance '250', called either the Barracuda or Starfire, according to specification, had been evolved from the very successful two-times World Moto-cross Championship-winning Victor Grand Prix; the 'light 500' roadster Victor had, for some obscure reason, been renamed the B44 441 cc Shooting Star, reviving an appelation that had formerly applied to the alloy engined 500 cc A7 type, discontinued in 1962. The 500 cc A50 twin-cylinder Royal Star and the single- and dual-carburettor 650 A65T Thunderbolt and A65L Lightning twins completed the programme. Alternative versions of the A65 machine, such as the Cyclone, Hornet, Spitfire and Firebird, had either been abandoned or were listed only for export.

Nevertheless, while the Small Heath top brass and the Umberslade Hall experimenters were busy in other directions, what was left of the old guard of motor-cycle men had quietly been at work on an engine specifically intended to satisfy the American call for silky superbikes. From the Meriden drawing office, Bert Hopwood, Doug Hele and Jack Wicks, who for long had been Edward Turner's chief design assistant, produced their plans for a three-cylinder machine that made its bow in 1968 — for export only; almost a year elapsed before it reached the home market.

Three-cylinder side-valve engines had powered some of the earliest Rolls-Royce cars, and there had been numerous triple-pot two-strokes, but the three-in-a-row four-stroke layout had had practically no development until the Italian MV-Agusta company, aided by their ace rider, Giacomo Agostini, had demonstrated so devastatingly what could be done with a 120-degree crankshaft. Whereas MV had produced their 'three' by removing one cylinder from their proven 'four', Hopwood achieved his by adding a cylinder to an established twin, the Triumph Tiger 100. The result is so well known to motorcyclists that a comprehensive description would here be superfluous; suffice to say that the 67 × 70 mm, 740 cc engine used the same valve arrangement as had been adopted by Edward Turner for his original 1937 Speed Twin — camshafts fore and aft athwart the cylinder block, operating pushrods enclosed in tubes. Three carburettors were used.

The crankshaft, forged in one plane, reheated and twisted to provide 120-degree throws, was balanced by bob-weights (no flywheel) and carried in a mixture of plain, roller and ball journals. A triplex primary chain drove a car-type diaphragm clutch in a separate dry compartment, and the four-speed box was bolted to the crankcase rear. Swing-fork rear suspension and 8-inch twin-leading-shoe brakes figured in the specification. The power output of the early types was 58 bhp at 7,250 rpm — 120 mph and a standing start acceleration figure of under 14 seconds over a quarter-mile. These results were greatly improved as development proceeded.

Sensibly, the new project was launched in two 'same, only different' forms. As the BSA A75 Rocket Three the engine, in a full-loop duplex-tube frame, had its cylinders inclined forward at a small angle. With the Triumph Trident the block was upright in a single front-down-tube frame. Both types of unit were made in the BSA shops at Small Heath and, at a later date, the Tridents also became slopers.

These exciting British 'threes' were an instant success and the racing versions, prepared by Doug Hele, exhibited no untoward teething troubles when they made their debuts on American tracks. In their first big test, the 1970 Daytona 200-mile Experts race, Tridents were placed second and third and in the following year Rocket Threes, ridden by Dick Mann and Don Emde, were first and third with Don Castro on a Trident between them. Mann averaged a record 104.7 mph over the Daytona road circuit and BSA Ltd and BSA Inc, who had combined to mount an impressive ten-rider squad, were well satisfied with the results, although their two English stars, Mike Hailwood (Rocket) and Paul Smart (Trident), both of whom had been leaders in the early stages, were sidelined with break-downs that in no way reflected any deficiency in design.

Another renowned British road racer, John Cooper, had also been active aboard Rocket Threes. He beat Agostini to win the Race of the Year and Race of the South classics and won the Ontario 250-mile event. Indeed, on circuits everywhere the BSA/Triumph èquipes were riding high on a sweeping success wave. Tridents began their celebrated reign in the Isle of Man Production and Formula 750 classes and at the Thruxton Grand Prix d'Endurance Ray Pickrell's winning Rocket Three beat Paul Smart's Trident by a whisker. Nigel Rollason and Clive Brown won the 500 cc class, finishing eighth overall, and sharing a Gold Star specially built in the Armoury Road comp shop. With it they also scored outright wins in the 1971 Spanish and Dutch 24-hour endurance races.

A new B50SS model, named the Gold Star 500, appeared but bore no resemblance to its illustrious Goldie forerunners. It had an 84 × 90 mm, 499 cc, upright, single-cylinder, unit-construction engine in a type of frame which, like those of the current 650 cc twins, embodied a large-diameter top tube that also served as an oil container. The layout was the product of the Umberslade Hall team and, being too tall and too heavy, was generally disliked, even after efforts had been made to reduce the seat height.

'Over the sticks' Jeff Smith continued to demonstrate his dominance. In the 1970 New Year Honours List his services to the sport of motor cycling had been recognised when he became a Member of the British Empire, the first competition rider other than a road racer to be so officially rewarded. Since joining the BSA team in 1953 he had remained loyal to the Birmingham marque, taking part in every major trial and winning a great many of them. He had won nine British scrambles championships and was world moto-cross champion in 1964 and 1965. He had raced in every country in Europe, and in Russia, the United States, Canada, Australia, New Zealand — and even in the Congo!

But, for Jeff Smith and all his hard-riding, hard-working colleagues, the end of the Armoury Road route to fame and fortune was in sight. The group had run into such serious financial trouble that, in July 1971, the Small Heath competitions department, for over half a century the spiritual home of so many famous men, was closed, and so far as BSA were concerned, factory participation in motor-cycle sport ceased forthwith and for ever.

Chapter 19

Farewell to Piled Arms

'Go, litel book, go litel myn tragedie' — *Geoffrey Chaucer*

From the Small Heath press office there was issued in May 1972 a document titled *The March of the Piled Arms*. It began with a summary of BSA history through more than a hundred years, listed some outstanding achievements, described post-war growth of the group and ended, under a sub-heading, 'The story to date', with a brief, brave attempt to explain away the calamitous situation with which the company was then confronted. The text of this concluding passage was as follows:

The spring of 1971 heralded a major crisis for the whole Group and a drastic change in the company's fortunes resulted in a trading loss of £3 million.

Briefly, it seems likely that the company had tried to do too much in too short a time. Added to this there was sales resistance to some features of the motor cycles announced in November 1970 and, as shareholders were told, errors of management contributed to the situation.

Despite the gloom and rumours which were rife at the time, by the end of the year the chairman, Lord Shawcross (a director since 1968) stated emphatically that the company was still very much in business. Barclays Bank provided finance amounting to £10 million and the company, under new chief executive Brian Eustace, rapidly set about reorganising itself for the fight back to profitability.

Motor-cycle manufacture, both BSA and Triumph was concentrated in the Meriden plant, activities on the Small Heath site including the production of motor-cycle engines and components, and sub-contract work for hydraulic and hydrostatic manufacturers, became the responsibility of the newly formed BSA Engineering Ltd.

Overcoming the crisis involved a large number of redundancies at all levels; assets such as the holdings in Alfred Herbert and SMC and some small peripheral companies had to be sold. In all, it was a traumatic experience for a company which had seemed so recently to be on the crest of a wave. Nevertheless, the company's 111 year history has included many crises, all of which were eventually surmounted . . .

What this statement did not disclose was the fact that for a considerable time before the spring crisis of 1971 the Piled Arms had been collapsing. Since the £3½ million record year of 1960 trading had been decreasing at such a rate that the books for 1970 had shown a loss of £8½ mill-

ion. The motor-cycle division manager, Lionel Jofeh, was retired in July 1971 and in the following November parent-board chairman Eric Turner resigned, being succeeded by Lord Shawcross.

The press office's references to 'errors of management' and 'sales resistance' glossed over some extraordinary blunders, probably the most disastrous of which was the introduction in mid-1970 of a tricycle device called the Ariel 3. BSA had aimed it at three classes of customers — housewives (it carried a 50 lb load of shopping), teenagers and commuters. It was really a moped with anti-falling-off properties and was conceived after an intensive market research campaign that encouraged the factory to invest vast sums in tooling up for world-wide sales at the rate of 2,000 units a week. In fact, only a few hundred of these trikes were sold, and the ill-advised exercise was reckoned to have lost the group some £2 million, besides raising the hackles of all Ariel aficionados who resented the application of so honourable a name to an unwanted mongrel that did not even have a British engine — its 50 cc unit was obtained from Holland.

'Trying to do too much in too short a time' well describes the frantic rescue attempt undertaken late in 1971 when, in an all-hands-to-the-pump operation, no fewer than 13 new or much-revised BSA/Triumph models were announced, literally with a flourish of trumpets, at a gala in London's Lancaster Hotel. Responsible for arranging this shindig was PRO Reg Dancer, who recalls: 'It could be called the group's last desperate throw to make a real impact on the market. For the first time in 19 years I had a reasonable budget — £15,000 for the launch and we had nearly 350 press and trade people for a show that included The Young Generation and Dave Allen! Then, after a truly magnificent launch, the factory had a hundred-and-one different production problems, missed the market both at home and in America, and towards the end of the year the roof started to fall in!'

Among the line-up of prototypes for 1972 production were several that never made it, the most surprising being a 350 cc double-overhead-camshaft twin that had come from Edward Turner's now freelance drawing-board. In BSA guise it was named the Fury; as a Triumph it was the Bandit. Without the benefit of any practi-

Replacing the A7 and Golden Flash types, BSA's ultimate, unit-construction vertical-twin design arrived in 1962. In 500 and 650 sizes, with single and dual carburettor systems, it was used in a wide variety of models through the last ten years of the company's life (Motor Cycle).

cal development, it was tooled up for production at great cost, and then abandoned. Even if it had proved to be a viable performer, one wonders what its fate would have been for the hey-days of the 'nifty three-fifty' had long since passed. Mopeds and small no-peds had replaced scooters for ride-to-work purposes; trials and scrambles were the province of potent, lightweight two-strokes; superbikes had risen into the 1,000 cc category. Yet the last 'catalogue' (a single, folded broadsheet) ever issued from Small Heath

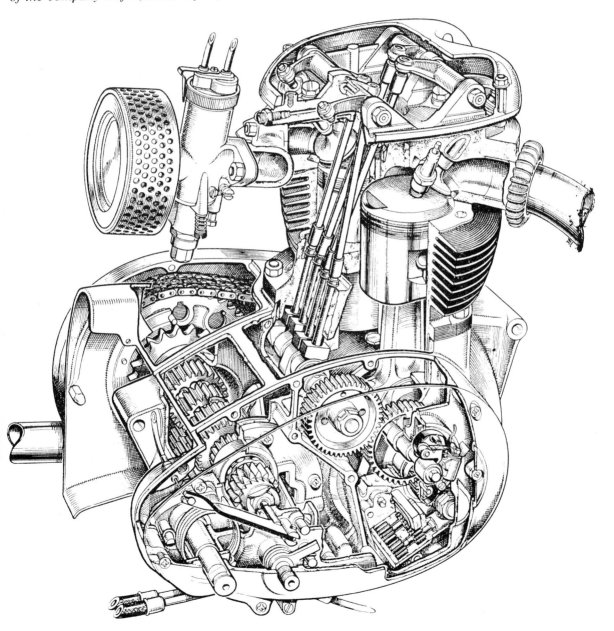

described a 1972/73 range that included none of these types — just four models, the Gold Star 500, the 650 cc Thunderbolt and Lighting twins and the 750 cc Rocket Three. Incredibly, even the evergreen Bantam, a 'popular favourite' if ever there was one, went into limbo.

Notwithstanding the bank's £10 million support and the sales of various assets, Lord Shawcross and a reconstructed board of directors were unable to prevent another multi-million pound loss and at the end of 1972 BSA was on the verge of bankruptcy.

During the ensuing months negotiations proceeded between the Department of Trade and Industry and Manganese Bronze Holdings, a company that had acquired the defunct Associated Motor Cycles concern and merged two of the industry's oldest marques into a Norton Villiers entity. The plan was that, with £10 million capital, part subscribed by the government and part by Manganese Bronze, a new company, Norton Villiers Triumph would be set up to make and market Norton and Triumph motor cycles.

BSA shareholders accepted the deal and in doing so finally toppled the Piled Arms, for manufacture of BSA machines formed no part of the NVT scheme, and sixty-three years of non-stop production ended abruptly in the summer of 1973.

The subsequent convulsions that ultimately engulfed the new regime are recounted by Harry Louis and Bob Currie in *The Story of Triumph Motor Cycles* and in the second edition of my own *Norton Story,* companions with this volume in the series of motor-cycling books published by Patrick Stephens Ltd.

A sad ending is a poor way in which to close such an heroic saga as that of BSA, and it would bring joy to many if we could say, as Winston Churchill did after the 1942 Battle of Egypt, 'This is not the end. It is not even the beginning of the end. But it is, perhaps, the end of the beginning'. Rumours of a revival of the marque crop up from time to time, but if ever there is a new breed of Beesas it is certain that they will not be sired in the old Small Heath citadel, for bulldozers and demolition gangs have ravaged the

squat, square Head Office, the New Building, the acres of workshops, the test track and the Armoury Road gates through which passed so many men and machines that made motor-cycling history.

Associations with that history are kept very much alive by, for example, that loyal band of enthusiasts, the BSA Owners' Club whose members all around the world lovingly cherish their Round Tanks, Slopers and Goldies (see Appendix B). Rocket Threes, painstakingly maintained, are still favourites with racing men. In the 1977 Isle of Man Formula One TT (won on a Honda by many-times-champion Phil Read at 97.02 mph) Malcolm Lucas brought his Rocket into fifth place at 92.06 mph, the first British machine to finish. Furthermore, he led the Midland MCRC's all-Rocket trio that took the club team prize.

Do these recollections make you wish you could go out and buy a brand-new BSA? You can, though it will be made, not in Birmingham, but in Nottingham, and you will have to pedal it. The Raleigh company perpetuated the trademark they acquired in 1956 and today the familiar winged-B transfer adorns some of the most aristocratic machines in the cycling world.

Remembering that it was by making bicycle fittings that BSA first entered into road transport, it might be apt to conclude with some sort of sententious remark about the tendency of wheels to turn in full circles. But there is a better, and perhaps more satisfying, way in which to contrive a happy ending. Somewhere in Birmingham, so runs a tantalising story, there is a tavern (could it be the 'Piled Arms'?) wherein the saloon bar has been redecorated with oak panelling salvaged from the Small Heath boardroom. If it exists, I'll find it, for surely there could not be a setting more redolent with nostalgia in which to pay a tribute to those pioneer directors, who themselves chose a Brummagem pub when they met on June 7 1861 to form The Birmingham Small Arms Company Limited.

Mister Chairman, the proposal before the Brotherhood of BSA is a toast . . . Here's to the memory!

Appendix A

BSA in the Clubman's TT, 1947-56

Junior and Senior races were run over four laps (151 miles) of the Mountain Circuit, except: (a) 1949, three laps (113 miles); (b) 1953 Senior, three laps; (c) 1955, nine laps (97 miles) of the Clypse Course; (d) 1956, three laps of the Mountain Circuit.

Except where otherwise indicated, all riders named were BSA-mounted.

1947

JUNIOR (4 laps): *23 entries, 21 starters, 4 on BSA.* Other makes: Norton, AJS, Triumph, Ariel, Excelsior, Matchless, Velocette. Fron Purslow 5th at 66.76 mph and Peter Moss, 7th. (Winner: Denis Parkinson, Norton, 70.74 mph). Others retired including J. W. Moore on lap 2 when lying 2nd.

SENIOR (4 laps): *33 entries, 23 starters, 2 on BSA.* Norton and Triumph predominant makes. Both BSAs (A7 twins) retired but Eric Stevens was 4th on lap 1. Eric Briggs (Norton) won at 78.67 mph from Allan Jefferies (Triumph) by 5 min 15 sec.

1948

JUNIOR (4 laps): *40 entries, 35 starters, 5 on BSA.* AJS (12) and Velocette (6) predominant. A. Klinge 21st (and last). Other BSAs retired, though Jack Difazio was 4th before lap 2 engine failure. Ronnie Hazlehurst (Velocette) won at 70.33 mph.

SENIOR (4 laps): *44 entries, 41 starters, 2 on BSA.* 1,000 cc Vincent-HRD, Norton and Triumph predominant. Jack Daniels won from Phil Heath at 80.51 mph both on Vincents. Both BSAs retired early.

1949

JUNIOR (3 laps): *85 entries, 74 starters, 21 on BSA.* Norton (14) AJS (10) Velocette (6). Harold Clark won at 75.18 mph from John Simister and Alan Taylor (both Nortons). Ray Hallett 4th and BSA also 11, 13, 15, 17, 19, 26, 29, 31, 33, 39, 47, 48, 52, 56 of 57 finishers. Only 5 BSAs retired, E. Harvey lying 2nd when a chain broke on the last lap. Clark knocked 50 sec off record lap, raising it to 75.81 mph.

Sensational debut for 350 Gold Stars and first of 8 successive Junior Clubman's victories.

SENIOR (3 laps): *55 entries, 43 starters, 4 on BSA.* Triumph (25) Norton (11). It was Geoff Duke's (Norton) year; won by 2.11 sec from Allan Jefferies (Triumph) at 82.97 mph. Jack Wright only BSA finisher, in 11th place.

1950

JUNIOR (4 laps): *100 entries, 93 starters, 41 on BSA.* Douglas 90-Plus (22) Norton (13). BSAs dominated race with first 4 places on laps 1 and 2 and first 3 on lap 3. After terrific struggle with Ken James, who retired on last lap, Brian Jackson won at 74.25 mph from Ian McGuffie with 'Buster' Brown (Norton) 3rd and John Clark (Douglas) 4th. Of 56 finishers BSA had 24 — 1, 2, 7, 8, 10, 12, 14, 17, 19, 21 (tied), 23, 24, 29, 30 (tied), 32, 33, 36, 39, 41, 42, 44, 50, 54, 56. Jackson raised lap record to 76.12 mph.

SENIOR (4 laps): *66 entries, 59 starters, 8 on BSA.* Triumph (28), Norton (16). At 75.60 mph Phil Carter (Norton) beat A. Hill (Triumph), followed by three more Nortons and two Triumphs. Best BSA Dave Bogie, 13th; others 15, 16, 17, 20, 24, 29, of 36 finishers. Only one BSA retired.

1951

JUNIOR (4 laps) *87 entries, 75 starters, 41 on BSA.* Douglas (16), Norton (9), AJS (4). Brian Purslow won at record 75.36 mph, hotly challenged by Nortons of G. E. Read, 2nd, ace-scrambler John Draper, 3rd, and Dave Bradshaw, 4th. Next BSA was Derek Farrant, 5th, another Norton 6th, a Douglas 7th, then BSAs 8, 9, 10, 11, 12, 13, 14, 15, 17, 18, 21, 22, 23, 24, 27, 28, 29, 30, 31, 32, 36, 37, 38, 40 — 26 of 41 finishers. 15 BSAs retired, as did 13 of 16 Douglases. Ken James set lap record at 76.55 mph before experiencing much trouble with his Norton and finishing last. BSA's dominance not yet quite total but very nearly so.

SENIOR (4 laps): *82 entries, 62 starters, 7 on BSA.* Norton (28), Triumph (20). Ivor Arber brought his Norton home 20 sec ahead of Ivan Wickstead (Triumph), at 79.70 mph. Best BSA Jack Wright 10th at 75.85 mph. Others 11, 25, 34, 36 out of 45 finishers; two retired. BSA impact on Senior Clubman's still virtually nil.

1952

JUNIOR (4 laps): *105 entries, 96 starters, 71 on*

BSA. Norton (14), Douglas (4). Eric Houseley led from start to finish, setting race record at 78.92 mph, 33.2 sec ahead of then unknown Bob McIntyre, who was 7.2 sec ahead of Ken James (Norton) with Charlie Staley and Derek Powell 4th and 5th. The only other places not taken by BSA were: Norton; 6 (Harry Plews), 9 (Bob Ritchie), 11 (John Clark), 26, 32, 36, 37, 44, 61. Douglas; 39 (Bernard Hargreaves), 48. AJS; 46. Matchless; 52, 54. Royal Enfield; 60 (Frank Sheene, Barry Sheene's father). With 47 of 64 finishers, 350 Gold Stars swept the board and Bob McIntyre did his last lap in 28 min 16.4 sec, 80.09 mph to knock 1 min 18.6 sec off Ken James's 1951 lap record.

SENIOR (4 laps): *94 entries, 87 starters, 15 on BSA.* Norton (34), Triumph (28). Bernard Hargreaves (Triumph) won at 82.45 mph from Nortons of Ken James, John Clark and Derek Farrant. Best BSA was Derek Powell, 8th, nearly 4 min behind the winner; others 14, 23, 24, 30, 34, 39, 51 among 60 finishers. Seven BSA retirements; Senior models not yet competitive.

1953

JUNIOR (4 laps) *73 entries, 70 starters, 53 on BSA.* Norton (12), AJS (2) Matchless (2), Douglas (1). Derek Powell won at record 80.17 mph with record lap at 80.96 mph. Jack Bottomley (Norton) fought strongly for second place but finished 3rd, 3.6 sec behind Owen Greenwood. BSAs took the next nine places and the only rivals to finish were: Norton; 3, 13, 23, 25, 27, 35, 45, 47, 48. AJS; 33. Apart from the gallant Bottomley, it was a BSA avalanche with 39 of the 49 finishers on Goldies.

SENIOR (3 laps): *62 entries, 58 starters, 7 on BSA.* Norton (25) Triumph (17). Bob Keeler won at 84.14 mph heading a Norton 1-2-3 with Eddie Crooks and Alan Holmes. Reduced to 3 laps through bad weather. BSAs finished 17, 21, 22, but one of the four retirements, Eddie Dow, had first demonstrated improved 500 Gold Star performance. He was only 21 sec behind the leader, Keeler, when he crashed heavily at Laurel Bank on the last lap. It was Dow's first Clubman's race and his second lap time was only 3 sec slower than Keeler's record 26 min 48 sec, 84.50 mph.

1954

JUNIOR (4 laps): *63 entries, 49 starters, 42 on BSA.* Norton (5), AJS (1), Douglas (1). A desperately exciting race. George Arnold led on lap 1 from joint seconds Phil Palmer and A. S. Bowie; 4th was Des Wright; 5th Geoff Tanner, on a lone Norton in the BSA den; 6th Jimmy Davie. Lap 2 even more exciting. Arnold still led from Bowie by

4 sec, with Davie a further 7 sec away in 3rd. Tanner had moved to 4th, Palmer was 5th and Jimmy Buchan 6th — 33 sec covering the leaderboard men. On lap 3 Davie was in the lead, 7 sec ahead of Bowie who was 19 sec ahead of Palmer, with Wright 4th, Tanner 5th and Arnold 6th. Palmer came through on the last lap to win at 81.83 mph (new record) by 12.4 sec from Wright, whose final lap was a record at 83.05 mph. Davie finished 3rd, Bowie 4th, Tanner 5th and Arnold 6th, 52.4 sec between the first six.

Of 41 finishers all were BSAs except: Norton; 5, 9, 34, 37, 39. Douglas; 23. AJS; 28. BSA scored 34 finishers and had 8 retirements.

SENIOR (4 laps): *46 entries, 39 starters, 12 on BSA.* Norton (14), Triumph (12). Nearly a clean sweep for the big 'Goldies', with Alastair King at 85.76 mph beating Ben Denton by 5.6 sec after Ewan Haldane had dropped from a race-long lead to 3rd berth. Tom Ovens (Triumph) was 4th and the BSAs of M. R. Baigent and Percy Tait (yes, *the* Percy Tait, of 'Slippery Sam' renown) completed the leader board. Alastair King knocked 47 sec off the lap record, lifting it to 87.02 mph. Other BSAs were: 10 (Eddie Dow), 14, 17, 18. Three retired. For the first time the Clubman's was taken out of Race Week and held on the previous Thursday, an unpopular move reflected in an entry decline.

1955

JUNIOR (9 laps, Clypse Course): *45 entries, 38 starters, 34 on BSA.* Norton (2), Douglas (1), Royal Enfield (1). Jimmy Buchan led from the start, winning, at 68.23 mph by 15.6 sec from the fast but spectacularly erratic Danny Joubert, from South Africa's Metropolitan Club, maker of the fastest lap at 69.78 mph. Peter Ferbrache, 2 min behind, was 3rd. BSA filled 29 of the 32 finishing places, missing only 28 (Norton), 29, 32 (Douglas). Five BSAs retired, including American Dave Hagan, the Mont' Christie Club's nominee.

SENIOR (9 laps, Clypse Course): *32 entries, 23 starters, 10 on BSA.* Triumph (10), Norton (3). On lap 1 Ian Atkinson and Ray Kelly shook the BSA legions by putting their Triumphs into 1st and 2nd places. Eleven seconds behind the leader came Eddie Dow in 3rd. Atkinson retained his lead on lap 2 but Dow was only 5 sec behind and he pulled ahead to win by 1 min 18 sec at 70.73 mph. Kelly held 3rd and Peter Ferbrache was 4th. A slow starter, Jim Drysdale later did four laps all under 9 min, a barrier not broken by any other rider. His best time, on laps 4 and 6, was 8 min 56 sec, 72.53 mph. BSA had 10 of the 20 finishers — 1, 4, 5, 6, 7, 10, 12, 14, 15, 16, and no retirements. The races were held on the Saturday before International Race Week, a little better than in 1954, but the use of the Clypse Course was largely responsible for the big drop in entries.

1956

JUNIOR (3 laps): *68 entries, 55 starters, 53 on BSA*. Norton (1), Velocette (1). A runaway win for Bernard Codd, who took a 34 sec lead on lap 1 over John Eckhart, which he stretched to 49.6 sec at the end to average 82.02 mph — a record despite machines having to carry almost full equipment, including lamps and silencers. Codd's best lap at 82.33 mph was only 15 sec more than Des Wright's 1954 record. Alan Shephard (Norton) was 3rd throughout and Eric Unwin, D. Jervis and James Morton were 4th, 5th, and 6th with only 13 sec between them. Except for John Righton (Velocette, 23rd) all the other finishers were on BSAs; five failed to finish, two having crashed.

SENIOR (3 laps): *42 entries, 32 starters, 24 on BSA*. Triumph (7), Norton (1). Barely 1½ hours after his Junior victory, Bernard Codd set off on another winning ride, being 27 sec ahead of Ron Jerrard after lap 1 and increasing his lead to 1 min 6.2 sec at the end, another record average, at 86.33 mph though his fastest lap at 86.52 mph was 9.4 sec slower than Alastair King's 1954 record. Tony Jenkins, D. Jervis, Fred Wallis and, after Jervis's retirement on lap 2, Dennis Smart, battled with Michael Brookes (Triumph) for leader board places. Fifth on lap 2, Brookes broke down on the Mountain and pushed and coasted in to finish 26th, thereby letting Australian G. Coombes into 6th place behind Jenkins, Wallis and Smart. Triumphs finished 7 (John Hurlstone), 19, 20, 22, 23, 25, 26,

and the lone Norton of B. F. Herbert was the last of the 28 finishers, 20 of them BSAs. Bernard Codd's 'double' was the only one achieved in the 10-year Clubman's series.

*　　　*　　　*

Renamed the Clubman's Trophy races, the 1956 events — Junior and Senior classes only — were something of an anti-climax, for they were staged on the Thursday after Race Week before an almost 'empty house'. Despite this loneliness for the short-distance runners (although back on the Mountain Circuit, the races had been cut to three laps) entries were well up on the depressed 1955 totals — perhaps because it was generally expected that this would be the last chance for an IoM outing. And so it proved, for the ACU, organising an ambitious Golden Jubilee TT programme, switched the club boys to Oulton Park for 1957, and never returned them to the Island.

*　　　*　　　*

Footnote Clubman's Gold Stars, some in standard form and some substantially modified and developed, also figured in large numbers in the International TTs and Manx Grands Prix. In 1955, for example, there were 16 in the Junior TT and no fewer than 30 in the Junior MGP and 27 in the Senior. A year later there were 22 Junior and 27 Senior MGP Gold Stars and 1957 saw 33 Junior and 19 Senior models in the September races, Goldie entries for which did not begin to fall off appreciably until 1961, when the type was nearing the end of its days and these faithful old war horses were no longer able to take the strain.

Appendix B

BSA Owners' Club

'BSA will never die — the BSA Owners' Club will see to that!'

With this defiant pledge as their battlecry, some 2,000 British and overseas enthusiasts keep their beloved marque alive and well. Collectively, they form the BSA Owners' Club, with a score of branches in the United Kingdom, affiliated groups in Australia, Czechoslovakia, France, Germany, Holland, Luxembourg, New Zealand, Tasmania and the USA, and individual members in practically every country in the world.

Membership is continually increasing and the scope of the Club's activities grows proportionately.

It was in Sheffield, in 1958, that a group of owners set up the first BSA one-make club. Others soon followed, in Nottingham, Birmingham and Surrey. By 1960 there were eight or nine such individual groups, all operating different sets of rules, subscription rates and 'aims and objects'. A National Committee had been established but its powers were so limited that it could do little more than keep the separate clubs in touch with one another.

In an effort towards unity, a magazine, called *Star*, was produced in January 1961. After a slow start, its influence gained momentum and, carrying the 'one for all' message, it greatly helped the National Committee to bring into being a recognised system of co-ordination. After many months of meetings between committees and delegates an extraordinary general meeting was held in October 1962, and massive support was given to the idea of a National BSA Owners' Club, to come into effect on January 1 1963, with a national form of rules and constitution, and standardised fees.

Since the taking of that step the BSAOC has become one of the biggest and most progressive of one-make motor-cycle clubs. In its own words it 'consists of enthusiasts from all over the world who have got together for their mutual benefit to enable them to participate in club life on international, national and local levels, to compete with riders of similar machines on equal terms, and discuss matters of common interest. AND, most important of all, since the closure of the BSA factory, to preserve the motor cycles we all love, which bear the great name of BSA.'

A major catalyst in BSAOC affairs is the *Star* magazine, nowadays a voluminous monthly publication that reaches every member. It covers a wide variety of subjects: general articles; hints and tips; reports from the branches and individual members; an overseas section; 'For Sale and Wanted' columns; and a 'Help or Breakdown' feature that lists members who can offer stranded owners assistance, accommodation, spares, or all three. Naturally, BSA owners help each other, but this directory supplies details of special services and telephone numbers.

Because of the growing number of overseas members the word 'National' was dropped from the Club's title in the 1970s, but the constitution was not changed. Each branch has its own rules within the framework of the National regulations, and from its own committee sends delegates to the Club's annual general meeting. Club membership carries an open invitation to any branch clubroom, where there are usually weekly meetings staging lectures, film shows, quizzes, darts matches and so forth. Some branches become involved with other local organisations, such as the RAC/ACU training scheme for learner riders.

Camping weekends, treasure hunts and visits to places of interest figure regularly in branch programmes and the highlight of outdoor activity is the BSA Clubs' International Rally, which is held in a different country each year at some venue where the majority of the European BSA clubs can meet for a week's holiday. Other important annual fixtures include the Isle of Man TT, the dinner-dance, usually at a Midlands hotel, and the annual general meeting.

Gatherings of the clan were few and far between in the 1960s, being mainly the Field Days held in the BSA factory's sports ground in Golden Hillock Road, Small Heath, where the works personnel acted as welcoming hosts and the company presented a number of splendid trophies for gymkhana-type competitions that are still contested to this day.

The BSAOC possesses a fine collection of cups, shields and trophies, of which the principal award is the Denis Parkinson Trophy, named for, and donated by, the Club's famous ex-road-racing president. It goes to the member with the highest total in a points-scoring system covering the year's competitive events. There is a counterpart for the best lady club member. The Freddie Frith Trophy is for the best score by a National member, that is, a club member who is not a branch member. One of the original BSA Field Day prizes is the Membership Shield, for the branch which enrols the largest number of new members. Another is the Attendance Trophy, for the branch with the highest average attendance at the various club events during the year.

Additionally, the Club has over 40 other prizes, won over the years, including the magnificent BSA/Triumph Group trophy awarded at the Big Three Rally, the British Motorcyclists Federation's Tug-o-War cup, won for three years in succession in the 1970s, and the recently won trophy for the Best Club Turnout at the 1976 Moto Club of Luxembourg Rally. The latest award was given to the Club by one of its vice-presidents, Andy Davies, formerly of the service reception department at the factory, who was always a friend to members when they visited Small Heath with their problems. It is awarded for the best Concours-condition BSA in the club.

The Club's prizes are always distributed at the annual dinner-dance, which, after a number of moves to different venues, is now held at the Strathallan Hotel, Birmingham.

Organising and expanding the social and competitive activities of the Club is one thing; maintaining ageing machines is an even more demanding preoccupation, and the BSAOC made one of its most useful and significant moves when, in 1975, it was decided to set up a Spares Scheme, on a separate membership-fee basis. The idea was to accumulate spare parts as and when BSA dealers offered them for sale and, eventually, to have parts that became unobtainable specially manufactured. To date, the operation has worked very well. The Scheme has bought some £2,000-worth of bits and pieces, has had manufactured transfers and other hard-to-get items, and has managed to acquire a considerable supply of materials at favourable trade discount prices. Every club member who enrols in the Spares Scheme receives lists of the items that are in stock, and the *Star* magazine serves to keep the lists up to date. Key man behind the Scheme is Barry 'Polly' Palmer, 244 The Cullerns, Haresfield, Highworth, Swindon, SN6 7NL, who is also the Club's Public Relations Officer. All information on joining is available from him, or from the Membership Secretary, Joe Fallon, 4 Elsham Drive, Worsley, Manchester, M28 5RU.

BSA will never die . . . book now for immortality!

Index